Ockeghem's
Missa cuiusvis toni

Publications of the Early Music Institute
Thomas Binkley, General Editor

Ockeghem's
Missa cuiusvis toni

In Its Original Notation and Edited in All the Modes

With an Introduction
by
George Houle

INDIANA UNIVERSITY PRESS
Bloomington and Indianapolis

M
2011
.03
C8
1992

The paper used in this publication meets the minimum standard
requirements of American National Standard for Information
Sciences—Permanence of Paper for Printed Library Materials,
ANSI Z39.48-1984.

™

Manufactured in the United States of America

Library of Congress Cataloging-in-Publication Data

Ockeghem, Johannes, d. 1496?
  [Missa cuiusvis toni]
  Ockeghem's Missa cuiusvis toni : in its original notation and
edited in all the modes / with an introduction by George Houle.
  1 score. — (Publications of the Early Music Institute)
  For 4 voices.
  "This edition provides parts for singers in mensural notation with
text underlay based on the Chigi Codex . . . A score and singer's
parts . . . in modern notation are provided in all four of the
authentic modes of Ockeghem's day"—P. [1].
  Includes bibliographical references.
  Contents: The Missa cuiusvis toni in the phrygian mode — The
Missa cuiusvis toni in the mixolydian mode — The Missa cuiusvis
toni in the lydian mode — The Missa cuiusvis toni in the dorian
mode.
  ISBN 0-253-32854-3
  1. Masses, Unaccompanied. I. Houle, George. II. Title.
III. Title: Missa cuiusvis toni. IV. Series.

M2011.03C8 1992   91-753671

1 2 3 4 5 96 95 94 93 92

Table of Contents

Introduction

Ockeghem's *Missa cuiusvis toni*, "mass in any mode," has continued to fascinate historians, theorists, and musicians from the time of its composition. It is one of Ockeghem's three freely composed masses notable for their subtle organizational devices. Its companions, the *Missa prolationis* and the *Missa mi-mi*, have been frequently performed, but the extraordinary beauty and variety of the *Missa cuiusvis toni* have yet to become fully known and appreciated. Solutions for its enigmatic title and notation have been offered by writers from Glareanus (1547) to the present day. This study offers the first comprehensive edition of the mass, and solutions that, it is hoped, will enable this work of art to take its rightful place in the performance repertory.

In this edition, singer's parts are provided in mensural notation with a text underlay based on the Chigi Codex[1] in order to encourage performance of the mass from its original notation. Scores and parts in modern notation are included in all the four authentic modes of Ockeghem's day. Measure lines, represented by small marks on the top line of each staff, are used in the modern notation edition; these are equivalent to the measure of the brevis in mensural notation. The parts in mensural and modern notation correspond note for note and page for page with measures numbered, so that singers may read the original notation and also have easy reference to the transcribed parts in each mode. The Lydian and Mixolydian modes are notated on their traditional pitches of f and g, the Phrygian and Dorian modes are transposed a fourth higher than their traditional pitches, to a and g, with one flat in their signatures.

The *Missa cuiusvis toni* is for four voices, written in Ockeghem's unmistakable style. The voices are rarely imitative of one another, although there are partial imitations and subtle reflections of musical ideas among them. When the listener becomes immersed in the freely unfolding melodic sequence of ideas in these independent voices, other music with pervasive melodic imitation can seem insistent and obvious by comparison. There is no *cantus firmus* and only the faintest suggestion of a motto in the initial rising curve of the soprano through the interval of a sixth that unifies the segments of the mass. There are relatively few cadences, and many of these are contradicted by overlapping voices so that long stretches of the music flow almost without interruption. This is a feature of Ockeghem's music that some consider to be almost mystical. Tempos vary, and these are specified by mensuration signs as well as by notation; the sections move from a slowly unfolding beginning through faster middle segments, then return to a slow tempo or rise to climactic quick movement. Textures are varied as well, there are changes from contrapuntal complexity to homophonic simplicity. Duets and trios emerge, and even solos seem to take place within the general four-voice texture. The only complete sections written for less than four voices are a duet for soprano and alto, *Benedictus*, and a trio for soprano, alto, and bass, *Qui venit*.

The relation of the music to the text is subtle and even elusive at times. Some phrases of the text are emphasized by homophonic texture, for instance *Qui tollis peccata mundi* in measure 32 of the *Gloria*. A shift of rhythm or an especially high note will at times underline a word or phrase, as at measure 21 of the *Gloria* where dotted minims in all parts give a different pace to the music at *Jesu Christe*, or at measure 26 of the *Sanctus* where the tenor rises through an octave on the word *gloria*. Just as quickly as these vivid moments arise their imagery dissolves into a less specific declamation or melodically flowing vehicle for the text. Intricate counterpoint offers its own fascination in some places, for instance in the *Amen* of the *Credo* at measure 182.

In the brief sections of the *Kyrie*, Ockeghem rarely writes for all four voices together. Duets between soprano and alto begin each section, the tenor joins, and finally the bass enters for the conclusion. In such an unusual work as this, it is possible to imagine that the composer first experimented with segments to see

1. Rome, Biblioteca Apostolica Vaticana, Chigi C.VIII.234.

whether they could be performed in all the modes, and of course, it is much simpler to write for fewer voices.

Writers from the 16th century (Glareanus,[2] Wilfflingseder[3]), 18th (Forkel[4]), 19th (Kiesewetter[5], Wooldridge,[6] Fröhlich,[7] Ambros,[8] Spitta,[9] Schlecht,[10]), and 20th centuries (Peter Wagner,[11] Kroyer,[12] Plamenac,[13] Levitan,[14] Perkins[15]) have commented on, or offered solutions to the clefless notation of this mass. Some of these solutions are useful and some are incorrect, but none of these writers offers a complete version of the mass in all modes. There is even uncertainty among music historians today about whether the *Missa cuiusvis toni* can actually live up to its title and be sung in all of the modes. Lewis Lockwood goes only as far as to write that it "can apparently be sung in any one of the four authentic-plagal pairs of modes in use at that time."[16] Some recent scholarship provides necessary clues to the interpretation of the mass, particularly Karol Berger's *Musica ficta*[17] which documents how chromatic inflections may be used to avoid forbidden note combinations that arise from the modal transformations of the mass.

Three topics require full consideration in order to understand the *Missa cuiusvis toni* and its performance. First is the structure of the music and its suitability for performance in different modes. Second is the emotional associations of the modes in the Renaissance. Third is the singer's technique of solmization, that allows the original notation to be interpreted in different modes and adjusted when non-harmonic clashes result from modal transformation.

For performers, the *Missa cuiusvis toni* can be regarded as a masterful pedagogical exercise offering both simple and complex problems of solmization. It may be a companion to Ockeghem's *Missa prolationis*, a composition that teaches singers how to read the complex notation of mensural canons, while the *Missa cuiusvis toni* teaches the modes through the hexachords of solmization.

For an audience, the subtle and pervasive modal transformation of melodies and counterpoints enhances the meaning of the familiar text. Repeated hearings lead to the perception of ever richer shadings of color within the emotional context of the mass. It is for us, as well as it was as for Renaissance listeners, an unparalleled exploration of modal transformation. It is hoped that the present edition will allow this fascinating and musically powerful work to reach a larger audience.

Structure of the *Missa cuiusvis toni*

The title, "mass in any mode" or "mass in whatever mode you will," makes a claim that may be difficult to understand. If the word "mode" were replaced by "key," the title would be quite clear in meaning,

---

2. Henricus Glareanus, *Dodecachordon*. Basel: 1547, reprinted 1969; tr. by Clement A. Miller, Musicological Studies and Documents, vol. VI. Rome: American Institute of Musicology, 1965.

3. Ambrosius Wilfflingseder, *Erotemata musices practicae*. Nuremberg, 1561, 66ff.

4. *Geschichte de Musik*, Vol. II, 535ff.

5. Raphael Georg Kiesewetter, *Verdienste der Niederländer*, Appendix, 25f; *Geschichte der Musik*, 1834, Appendix, xviii.

6. *Oxford History of Music*, vol II, 217ff.

7. *Beiträge zur Geschichte der Musik*, vol II, 124 and 126.

8. A. W. Ambros, *Geschichte der Musik*, vol. III. Leipzig, 1868, 177ff., rev. O. Kade, 1893, vol. 5, 1ff.

9. *Vierteljahrschrift für Musikwissenschaft*, vol. VI (1890), 142.

10. Raimund Schlecht, *Geschichte der Kirchenmusik*, Regensburg, 1871, 81ff.

11. Peter Wagner, *Geschichte der Messe*, Leipzig, 1913, 102ff.

12. *Festschrift Guido Adler*, 1930, 111.

13. Johannes Ockeghem, *Collected Works*, vol. I, xxvi-xxxi, 44-56.

14. Joseph S. Levitan, "Ockeghem's Clefless Compositions," *The Musical Quarterly*, xxiii (1937), 440-64.

15. Leeman L. Perkins, "Modal Strategies in the *Missa cuiusvis toni*," forthcoming in a festschrift for Patricia Carpenter.

16. "Mass" §II, 6, *The New Grove Dictionary of Music and Musicians*. London: Macmillan, 1980, vol. 11, 785.

17. Karol Berger, *Musica ficta: Theories of accidental inflections in vocal polyphony from Marchetto da Padova to Gioseffo Zarlino*. Cambridge: Cambridge University Press, 1987.

but listeners would expect to discern little but a difference of pitch between different versions. In our era of equal temperament, not even the particular qualities that different keys possess in mean-tone or well-tempered tunings would be evident.

If we were to understand "mode" to indicate either the modern minor or major mode, we would expect performances in these modes to have structural differences as well as changes of sonority and effect upon the emotions. It is interesting to hear the same musical ideas in minor coloring compared to that of the major, but the major and minor modes are, in a sense, opposites of one another. A continuous presentation of opposites may become predictable and annoying once the basic pattern is evident. Were we to attempt the performance of this mass in "either minor or major mode," there would be changes of pitch relationships among the notes rather than a uniform transposition of all notes to another pitch level. Performers today would expect the composer to specify just what the notes should be in each version in order to guarantee a reliable translation of the mass from one mode to another.

The modes in the fifteenth century were different from our major and minor modes. There were eight; four authentic and four plagal, each with its characteristic range, intervals, and cadential tones. Theorists from the eleventh through the seventeenth centuries associated emotional qualities with each of these modes. The earliest of these writers drew on emotional qualities related to various plainchants, but the writers of the late fifteenth and sixteenth centuries, influenced by humanistic scholarship, assigned emotional qualities to the modes as specified by ancient Greek theorists. They relied less on textual settings in chant or on observation of the effect of the modes on listeners.

Each fifteenth-century mode was based on a characteristic interval of a fifth. Four different fifths can be distinguished by the placement of a semitone among the tones that make up the interval. If the semitone is between the second and third tones from the lowest note, the fifth is the first species. If the semitone is between the first and second tones, it is the second species, if between the third and fourth tones, it is the third species, and if between the fourth and fifth tones it is the fourth. The lowest tone of the fifth is the finalis of the mode, the upper note of the fifth is usually the dominant of the mode amongst the authentic modes, but the Phrygian dominant is an exception: it is a sixth above its finalis. There are only three species of fourths, also distinguished by the position of a semitone among the tones. The first species of fourth places the semitone in the middle, the second species places it between the first and second tones, and the third places it between the third and fourth tones. These fourths and fifths are illustrated in Example 2 on page 25.

The modes are organized in authentic-plagal pairs that share the same intervals but differ in range. Example 2 also shows the pitches and intervals of the eight modes of Ockeghem's time. The protus pair (the first and second modes called Dorian and Hypodorian) share the first species of fifth and fourth. The deuterus (the third and fourth modes, Phrygian and Hypophrygian) share the second species of fifth and fourth. The tritus (fifth and sixth modes, Lydian and Hypolydian) share the third species of fifth and fourth, and the tetrardus (seventh and eighth modes, Mixolydian and Hypomixolydian) share the fourth species of fifth but must borrow the second species of fourth in order to complete their range. Heinrich Glareanus added four more modes to these eight in 1547: Æolian and Hypoæolian, Ionian and Hypoionian. These became accepted in the second half of the sixteenth century, but were not recognized in Ockeghem's time.[18]

The mode of a composition was usually considered to be that of the tenor part, and established by its range and intervals. Musical theory specified ideal intervals and ranges for each voice, but compositional practice ultimately defined the modes and their intervals. Modal compositions were often mixtures of melodic structures, for which the term *commixtio* was used in both monophonic and contrapuntal textures. Certain modes were frequently mixed together, a discussion of this occurs in Glareanus's *Dodecachordon* with numerous examples. Cadences may occur on many of the tones of a mode, not just the finalis, without

---

18. The article on "Mode" by Harold Powers in *The New Grove Dictionary of Music and Musicians*, ed. by Stanley Sadie (London: Macmillan, 1980), vol. 12, 384-412, is an excellent and thorough introduction to this subject.

weakening the fundamental order. As a result, modality is more subtle, various, and loosely structured than tonality.

Bernhard Meier has examined a large repertory of fifteenth- and sixteenth-century compositions in order to identify the musical ranges and cadence plans in authentic and plagal modes. He compares the practice of composers with the ideal organizations suggested by theorists,[19] and reports "the nature of every mode that is represented by final and melodic range in tenor and soprano is also revealed by a characteristic cadence plan,"[20] which he then sets forth for each mode. Although the conclusions cited here are much simplified from Meier's chapter, the basic outline remains. The Mixolydian modes 7 and 8, for instance, are identified by the use of the fourth species of fifth, g' to d'' in the soprano and at the lower octave in the tenor. The plagal mode is identified by use of the fourth d' to g' rather than d'' to g'' which characterizes the authentic. Cadences on g (modal finalis) and d (modal dominant or *repercussa*) are characteristic of mode 7, and on g and c (the modal *repercussa* in the plagal) for mode 8, together with a few cadences on other degrees that may be used to emphasize a word or for variety.

In the Dorian modes the ranges of soprano and tenor are dominated by the first species of fifth and fourth in the octave from d' to d'' for the authentic, and these same intervals in the octave from a' to a'' for the plagal (although the plagal Dorian is usually transposed up a fourth, and sometimes an octave higher to suit vocal ranges). In authentic Dorian, the cadences are most frequently on d and a, less frequently on f, g, c and b-flat. In plagal Hypodorian the most frequent cadences are on d and f, with less frequent cadences on g, c, and a.

For the Lydian modes 5 and 6, Meier comments that the signature of b-flat is used when the final is f, as is acknowledged by most theorists. This makes the Lydian intervallic structure identical to that of Glareanus's Ionian and Hypoionian modes. The ranges of soprano and tenor are dominated by the fourth species of fifth (because of the b-flat signature) and the third species of fourth in the octave from f' to f'' in the authentic, and in the octave from c' to c'' in the plagal mode. The cadences of the Lydian mode are on the modal finalis f and the fifth above, c, the dominant. The third ranking cadence is on a, and cadences may be found on other degrees as well. In the Hypolydian, the primary cadences are on f and a, with the third most important cadence on the c below the finalis.

The Phrygian modes 3 and 4 were special cases. Plagal Phrygian melodies generally did not occupy their theoretically specified modal octave from b to b', but used a range from c to c' instead. The melodic range did not clearly differentiate between Phrygian and Hypophrygian but the relation of finalis to dominant, the *repercussio*, did. The Phrygian cadences of greatest importance are those on e and a, not those on c, the modal dominant a sixth above the finalis. Hypophrygian cadences place greater emphasis on e and g, with fewer cadences on a and d, the tone below the finalis.

Ockeghem's title, "mass in any mode" suggests not only that it might be performed in all modes but that it is organized by a plan common to the modes. This would seem to be impossible because of the important differences among the modes. Modality is more loosely organized than tonality, as noted before, but because of this each mode depends on its unique characteristics for its identity. Perhaps we may interpret "any" mode as "any authentic" or "any plagal" mode? There are points in common between all authentic modes, for example, the soprano and tenor ranges most characteristic of all the authentic modes are an octave from the finalis upward. Three authentic modes, Dorian, Lydian, and Mixolydian, all have their most important cadences on the finalis and dominant, a fifth apart. In the Phrygian mode the important cadences are on the finalis and fourth degree rather than on the sixth degree, the dominant. Important

19. Bernhard Meier, *The Modes of Classical Vocal Polyphony Described According to the Sources*, with revisions by the author, tr. by Ellen S. Beebe. New York: Broude Brothers Ltd., 1988. A translation of *Die Tonarten der klassischen Vokalpolyphonie*. Utrecht: Oosthoek, Scheltema & Holkema, 1974. See chapter 5, "Musical ranges and cadence plans of the authentic and plagal modes," 123-70.

20. Meier, 128.

cadences in the plagal modes are a third apart, except in the Hypodorian where they are at the interval of a sixth. It would seem that a composition that desires to amalgamate most of the characteristics of the modes would necessarily utilize characteristics shared by most of the authentic or plagal modes.

Leeman Perkins has discussed the organization of the *Missa cuiusvis toni* in a perceptive article that shows the surprising choices that Ockeghem made in the work.[21] The most frequent cadences (29) are on the fourth degree of the mode and the next most frequent (25) are on the finalis. Then there are 3 cadences on the fifth, 3 on the sixth, and 2 on the third degree of the mode. These choices are most consonant with the Phrygian mode and coincide scarcely at all with the other three authentic modes. The ranges of the parts offer another view of modal organization. Perkins writes "if one were to rely on Tinctoris's rule of thumb and identify the mode of the polyphonic work overall with regard to the tenor, the *Missa cuiusvis toni* exemplifies essentially the authentic mode based on each of the four traditional finals. It may be, nonetheless, that it was also Ockeghem's intention to illustrate modal mixture, combining authentic and plagal ranges in the superius, on the one hand, and placing the plagal Credo as a pivot of sorts between the authentic sections on either side."

The reasons behind Ockeghem's choice of Phrygian intervals for his mass can be found in the composition of cadences. The cadence formula common to the finalis of the Mixolydian, Dorian, and Lydian modes cannot be transposed unchanged to the Phrygian, but a Phrygian cadence may be transposed to the other modes. Cadences in the Phrygian mode are difficult to write because of the potential diminished fifth between B and f that would occur between the penultimate notes in the bass and either tenor or alto voices. This is illustrated in the first line of Example 1 where the same cadence is transposed to different modes. In Mixolydian and Dorian the tone below the finalis must be raised by the customary semitone, a normal adjustment for performers to make, and in Lydian no change is necessary.

21. Leeman Perkins, "Modal strategies."

In the Phrygian transposition of this Mixolydian cadence there is a diminished fifth between the penultimate notes in the bass (b-*mi*) and tenor (f-*fa*), a discordant harmonic interval that must be changed to a perfect fifth. The normal adjustment of this interval requires that b-*mi* be changed to b-*fa*, lowering it a semitone by a flat. This adjustment is precluded here because it would create another forbidden interval, an augmented fourth (or tritone) in the linear progression of the bass b-flat to e-natural.[22] A less usual correction of the tritone would be to raise the f-*fa* a semitone by a sharp, this solves the harmonic conflict but destroys the characteristic intervals of the Phrygian cadence, the semitone descent in the tenor against a rising tone in the soprano. Phrygian cadences must be constructed quite differently in order to avoid these problems.

The second line of Example 1 shows a Phrygian cadence[23] in four voices transposed to other authentic modes. When appropriate cadential *musica ficta* is added, we will hear augmented fourths between the penultimate notes of the soprano and alto in Mixolydian (c to f-sharp) and Dorian (g to c-sharp). If the Lydian mode is written with a b-flat signature, a possibility that will be discussed later in this introduction, the cadence will have an augmented fourth between b-flat in the alto and and e in the soprano. These augmented fourths are resolved by linear progressions to the nearest semitones, resolutions that excuse the harmonic dissonance to the ear. It is possible to transpose most four-voice Phrygian cadences to the other modes, but not the reverse. This particular cadence is not as resonant as it might be because of the disguised parallel unisons between the tenor and alto, and could perhaps be improved.

Line three of Example 1 offers examples of technically excellent Phrygian cadences. The first, by Sixtus Dietrich,[24] is in three voices, which are much more easily brought to a cadence in the Phrygian than four. The cadential resolution sounds the interval of a fifth above the finalis and there is no falling fifth or rising fourth in the bass. The second, by Heinrich Isaac,[25] in four voices, has a falling fourth to a in the bass; to modern ears this is a "plagal" cadence to the wrong bass note, apparently the root of a chord on a. To Renaissance ears the cadence is made by the progression of the soprano and tenor, a major sixth that expands to an octave e, and the other voices accompany the cadence with full sonority. This Phrygian cadence cannot be transposed to the other modes. The final example is Ockeghem's Phrygian cadence to the finalis of the mode, composed with care for the full sonority of four voices. This cadence has clearly been composed for the Phrygian finalis, but can be transposed to the finalis tones of the other three authentic modes.

Cadences to degrees of the mode other than the finalis in the *Missa cuiusvis toni* have a variety of forms, but do not always avoid the falling fifth or rising fourth in the bass. Transformations of these from the Phrygian to other authentic modes, one tone up, one tone down, or a third higher, will not place them on the Phrygian intervals, except for the three cadences to the sixth degree of the mode when the modal finalis is g, Mixolydian. These must be altered by raising the diminished fifth, b to f, by an f-sharp as was suggested above for the example at the end of line 1. They remain cadences to the sixth degree of the Mixolydian mode, but are not Phrygian in their intervals.

The prominence of cadences on the fourth degree of the mode is a Phrygian characteristic. There are very few cadences to the fifth degree of the mode, which we might expect to be the most frequent cadential tone for the other authentic modes. This is a necessary condition if the mass is to be performed in Phrygian, because cadences to b, the fifth degree of the Phrygian mode, must be as carefully calculated as those to e.

22. A tritone is an augmented fourth, equal to the sum of three whole tones. In equal temperament it is identical in sound to a diminished fifth, but in voice leading, these intervals are treated quite differently. A distinction will be made in this introduction between a tritone or augmented fourth and a diminished fifth, calculated from lower to higher pitches. Altered pitches (*musica ficta*) will be affected by this distinction.

23. The original of which is found on page 394 of the second volume of Clement Miller's translation of Glareanus's *Dodecachordon*, a cadence in "Elegy of the Holy Magdalene at the Tomb of the Lord" by an anonymous composer.

24. from the *Dodecachordon*, tr. by Clement Miller vol. 2, 349.

25. from the *Dodecachordon*, tr. by Clement Miller, vol. 2, 337.

The only neutral modal feature of the mass may be that of the ranges of the parts, and even then the Phrygian mode is often evident, particularly in the tenor.

The *Missa cuiusvis toni* can most easily be performed in the Phrygian and Mixolydian modes, it is more difficult to sing in the Lydian, and it is a serious test of any performer's solmization technique in the Dorian mode. It illustrates the flexibility of the modal system simply because it can be performed in different modes, but to a musician steeped in the differences of structure of the modes, it is most perfectly suitable to the Phrygian.

There are two compelling reasons for Ockeghem to have composed this puzzle mass: to explore the emotional connotations of the modes, and to invent a supreme test of a singer's command of solmisation technique. The modes were linked with moral and emotional responses in the minds of medieval and Renaissance musicians, and a single composition that can take on the character of four different modes illustrates these responses as no other work can.

Emotional Connotations of the Modes

"The modes were fascinating to Renaissance musicians not simply because they were a link to a noble ancient past but because they were thought to unlock the powers of music over human feelings and morals."[26] The modes were loosely based on ancient Greek musical theory which was little enough known to medieval musicians that the modes were in effect newly created and quite different from their supposed models. The medieval codification of plainchant by modal categories was an order imposed on an already existing repertory of music, for the most part, and therefore an explanation after the fact. The emotional power of the modes, derived from Plato's *Republic*, *Laws*, and Aristotle's *Politics*, was first systematically described by Renaissance musical theorists such as Gaffurio in the late fifteenth century. Changes in the theory of modes during the fifteenth and sixteenth centuries derived from an increasing knowledge of ancient Greek musical theory as well as from the aural perception of music.

Theorists imbued withe the spirit of Renaissance humanism enjoined composers to choose the right mode for a particular text as the most authoritative means to a proper interpretation. We may question whether it is the mode or the text that sways the listener, but a musical tradition was established by a generation of composers who followed the precepts of these theorists, and their music often vividly exemplified these humanist ideas.

Theorists disagreed about which emotion should be attributed to a mode but all accepted the idea that the musical modes conveyed or embodied emotional states. How might the suitability of emotional attribution be judged? Ancient authors were most frequently cited as the authority for emotional associations of the modes, but Glareanus mentions that a great composer such as Josquin Des Prez was able to convey a particular emotion in a mode different from that ascribed to it by tradition because of the power of his art. Performers can create or increase an emotional state by their interpretation, and it is possible that a theorist's characterization of the modes gave them their essential clues. Singers can find the basis for various interpretations in theorists' descriptions of the modes and thereby refresh repeated performances.

Phrygian

The Phrygian mode is less frequently used for settings of the mass than other modes, perhaps because of its emotional connotations. In the mid-11th century, Hermannus Contractus called the Phrygian "excited or leaping," and Frutolfus of Michelsburg at the end of the 11th century called it "excitable." Johannes Afflighemensis, at the about the same time, said the Phrygian was "harsh and rather indignant leaping

---

26. Claude V. Palisca, *Humanism in Italian Renaissance Musical Thought*. New Haven: Yale University Press, 1985, 12.

about."[27] In Gaffurio's writings at the end of the fifteenth century, the range of emotional effects of the mode is considerably expanded: "the Phrygian mode is depicted in a fiery color (as it provokes a greater movement of bile), for it is believed that it is appropriate to harsh and severe men in exciting them to anger. The cause of this is the very high whole tone above its two conjunct tetrachords as it moves forcibly with the speed of a high sound. It is said that with this mode, which uses the anapest, the Lacedemonians and Cretans were easily incited to war. Their army was not accustomed to descend to battle before they were aroused by the sound of the tibia and the movement of the anapest; by this sound they were reminded to strike the enemy forcibly with powerful and repeated blows. At a banquet of Alexander, Timotheus aroused the king with Phrygian music to arm himself. A drunken Tauromenian youth, whom Boethius recalls in the prologue of his *Musica*, was incited by the Phrygian sound and hastened to burn down a house."[28]

Ramos de Pareja echoes many of the same qualities of the mode, the Phrygian "incites to anger, and is harsh. Its humour is choler, its planet is Mars, its muse is Erato, and its color is fiery."[29] Ornithoparcus, translated by John Dowland, differs: "others take pleasure in the seuere, & as it were disdainful stalking of the third," but then, quoting Cassiodorus he writes, "the Phrygian causeth wars, and enflameth fury".[30] Juan Bermudo continues in the same interpretative tradition, writing that it is "severe, provocative to anger. Its symbolic planet is Mars. It suits proud, angry, cruel ideas, and those who delight in these. It induces animosity and choler and is suitable for texts of spiritual or temporal battles."[31]

Glareanus is the first to ascribe a completely different character to the mode, one more evident in the music of sixteenth-century composers. "This mode has a certain mournfulness and . . . it excites the emotions to lamenting." He goes on to admit the traditional connotations, "some say that it evokes the harsh reviling of the indignant, others say it incites to battle and enflames the appetite of a frenzied rage."[32] Aggression and lamentation might be seen as paired opposites, as brutality and sentimentality. Zarlino describes the intervals of the mode rather than ancient authority as the cause of its emotional force: "if it cadences on A instead of B-natural it is mixed with the ninth mode with which it shares the second species of fourth. It goes well with words that cause weeping, such as laments."[33]

The somewhat harsh and highly colored emotions thus described for the Phrygian are not ideal evocations for the Ordinary of the Mass, but rather for the Requiem or particular motet texts. Because of this, Ockeghem's choice of the basic structure of Phrygian mode for this mass seems to be less for the emotional significance than for the compositional requirements of its intervals. If the text of the mass can be regarded as inherently neutral or variable in its emotional content, it is fascinating to hear this composition in its various modal emotional affects.

---

27. All three are quoted in Harold Powers article "Mode" in *The New Grove Dictionary of Music and Musicians*, ed. by Stanley Sadie. London: Macmillan, 1980, vol. 12, 398.

28. *De Harmonia Musicorum Instrumentorum Opus*. Milan: Gotardus Pontanus Calographus, 1518, tr. by Clement A. Miller, Musicological Studies and Documents 33. Rome: American Institute of Musicology, 1977, 183.

29. *Musica practica*. Bologna: Baltasar de Hiriberia, 1482. Ed. by Johannes Wolf. Publikationen der Internationalen Musikgesellschaft 7 (1924-25), 13-20.

30. *Musicae active Micrologus*. Leipzig: 1517, tr. by John Dowland as *Andreas ornithoparcus His Micrologus, or Introduction: Containing the Art of Singing*. 1609. Reprinted and ed. by Gustave Reese and Steven Ledbetter as *A Compendium of Musical Practice*. New York: Dover, 1973.

31. *El libro llamado declaración de instrumentos musicales*. Osuna: 1555.

32. Heinrich Glarean, *Dodecachordon*. Basel: Heinrich Petri, 1547. Trans. and ed. Clement A. Miller. Musicological Studies and Documents 6. 2 vols. Rome: American Institute of Musicology, 1965.

33. *Le Istitutioni harmoniche*, Venice: 1558. Part III tr. by Guy A. Marco and Claude V. Palisca as *The Art of Counterpoint*, New Haven: 1968; New York 1976, 1983. Part IV tr. by Vered Cohen as *On the Modes*, ed. by Claude A. Palisca, New Haven: 1983, 324.

Mixolydian

Hermannus called the Mixolydian "garrulous," Frutolfus called it "joyful and merry," and Johannes says that it has "theatrical leaps."[34] Gaffurio has this to offer: "the Mixolydian has a twofold nature since it contains the lowest tetrachord of the Dorian mode and the highest whole tone above in the two conjunct tetrachords. It has the nature of excitement and of continence; for this reason painters show it in a mixed color. They say that in various dances (those that are more excited and those recalled to sorrow) it prefigures the customs of adolescents and the young. There are those who believe that the modes participate in celestial harmony. They say the sun rules the Dorian, and ascribe the Phrygian to Mars, the Lydian to Jupiter, and the Mixolydian to Saturn." Most of this is echoed by Ramos de Pareja, "it is light and jocund, and accords with a semi-crystaline color. Its humour is melancholy, its planet is Saturn, and its muse is Polyhymnia."

Ornithoparcus ascribes yet another character to it: "the warlike leapings of the seventh." Zarlino mixes Gaffurio's and Ornithoparcus's characterizations: "(it) accompanies words or matters that are light, merry, and also those signifying menaces, perturbations and wrath."[35]

Glareanus, as the first theorist to recognize the Ionian and Æolian modes, transferred compositions to the new modes that had hitherto been considered either Mixolydian or Dorian. "[The Mixolydian] was in very great use among early church musicians but in our time the Mixolydian and its plagal are almost unknown. I think this has occurred because the Ionian, a more celebrated mode and as I believe, older in men's usage, has the fifth, ut-sol in common with the Mixolydian. It has a certain tranquil dignity which both moves and dominates the people."

Bermudo treats the Mixolydian as a mixture of characteristics, some quite opposite to the others. "(Its) planet is Saturn and its humour is melancholy. It is sad and lazy, but also has to do with lasciviousness or lightness, and joy. It invites both good and bad. Texts agreeing with those for the 3rd, 4th, 5th, and even the 8th modes will be used with this mode. Words that signify ceremony belong to this."

Lydian

Hermannus called the Lydian "voluptuous," Frutolfus "joyful," and Johannes ascribed to it a "moderate wantonness and a sudden fall to the final." Gaffurio detailed the authoritative references that gave the Lydian its reputation. "The Lydian mode (as some say) offers a pleasing sound to those who are very agreeable and jovial in nature. Thus it is said that the Lydians, jovial and agreeable by nature, were pleased by melodies of the same sort, which are comparable to a blood-red color. The Tuscans proceeding from the Lydians, followed their choral dances. Not only is the mode said to fit joviality and pleasure, but it is far from the modesty of the Dorian (as it is higher) and the severity of the Phrygian. It is believed by many to fit weeping and lamentation, emotions for whose sake it was formed originally. Olympus played the pipe in the Lydian mode at the funeral rites of Pytho, and therefore such performers are called *siticines* or funeral musicians. According to Boethius it was customary with the ancients to precede the music of the piper with lamentations, just as Papinius Statius testified in this verse: "The pipe with a curved horn brays lowly, to which the shades of children were usually led in a funeral procession." They were accustomed to do this in the Lydian mode, and while weeping the mourners sang their sorrow (which is especially feminine), so that with such a song it became sweeter through the weeping."

Ramos de Pareja emphasizes only the bright and cheerful side of Gaffurio's characterization. "It is merry, delightful, pleasant, and sanguine. It destroys sadness and anxiety, and is depicted in blood color. Its symbolic god is Jove, and it depicts good fortune and generosity. Its muse is Euterpe." Bermudo is in

---

34. Powers, 398.
35. Zarlino, 327.

agreement with Ramos, "The fifth mode is sanguine, its planet is Jupiter. It is optimistic, benevolent, gentle, joking. Augustine calls it delightful, happy, modest. It will express texts of happiness, joy, reports of victory." Ornithoparchus modifies this, but retains a positive character: "others are moued by the modest wantonness of the fift." (Quoting Cassiodorus) "The Lydian doth sharpen the wit of the dull, and doth make them that are burdened with earthly desires to desire heauenly things, an excellent worker of good things. . ." Zarlino modifies this still more: "it is used to express joy and solace to troubled souls and is ecclesiastical, not much used by secular composers."[36]

Glareanus discriminates between the Lydian mode on f with a b-*mi* and the same mode with a b-*fa*, or b-flat. In his system the Ionian mode was identical to the Lydian with a b-*fa*, and some distinction had to be made between them. "This mode was in great use among early church musicians. . . but the mode seems harsh, and Lucian calls it Bacchic, Apuleius, plaintive. I consider the Lydian an excellent mode if one would treat it as the early church musicians did (i.e. with b-*mi*) . . . yet one rarely finds a pure Lydian in which Fa has not been introduced somewhere. The Ionian is more natural than the Lydian, but the Lydian is more dignified."

Dorian

Hermannus calls the Dorian "serious or noble," Frutolfus writes that it is "mobile because it is capable of all affects," and Johannes comments on its "lingering and courtly meanderings." Gaffurio says "In the more serious matters the ancients admitted only the Dorian mode since they truly loved its perpetual constancy and severity. They did not approve anything deceitful or occult but anything simple and open . . . So Plato admired the virile and serious Dorian music; the soft and effeminate music introduced later he said should be disdained . . . Plato approved and admitted the Dorian harmony because it combined fortitude and temperance. Nature has compared various human associations with the four modes. The Dorian is very appropriate for more serious mental dispositions and bodily movements, and was considered by the seers as the mover of phlegm. In the same way it was appropriate to distinguished men of talent, and its representation was given to painters in a color very similar to crystaline . . . Thus the ancients extolled the Dorian mode as the leader of a correct and good manner of living, and as a teacher of extraordinary value."[37] Bartolomé Ramos de Pareja agrees with this, but in a much shorter form. "The attributes of Dorian are a crystal color, which is changeable towards all affections; its planet is the sun which dries wetness, its humor is phlegmatic, and its Muse is Melpomene."[38]

Ornithoparcus writes "some are delighted with the crabbed and courtly wandring of the first tone. Cassiodorus says, 'The Darian moode is the bestower of wisedome and causer of chastity . . .' Plato alloweth of the Dorian, both because it is manly & also doth delight valiant men, & is a discouerer of warlike matters."

Glareanus offers it a character based on ancient authority: "this mode is called grave by Lucian, martial by Apuleius, dispenser of prudence and producer of purity by others. Some say it moves morosely and in a dignified way. The Dorian presents a certain majesty and dignity which is easier to admire than to explain."[39] Juan Bermudo relies on Cicero's *de Republica* as an authority. He compares the Dorian to the sun, because of its dominion over all other modes, and over phlegm. "The phlegmatic man will be awakened to joy. It is suitable to intelligent and manly things. Composers who use the Dorian are of good judgment and eloquent. Happy texts are suitable to this mode."

Zarlino uses musical intervals themselves as the basis of his characterization of the mode: "it has a certain medium effect between sad and cheerful (*mesto & allegro*). On account of the minor third in the

---

36. Zarlino, 325.
37. Gaffurio, 180-81.
38. Ramos de Pareja, *Tractatus Tertius, Capitulum Tertiam*, 56.
39. Glareanus, 182-83.

concentus on the the two extreme notes of the fifth and of the fourth, and not having a major third in the low register it is by nature somewhat sad. However by accidental movement we can accommodate it to words that are full of gravity and deal with lofty and sententious concepts."[40]

The Renaissance humanist ascriptions of emotions to the modes were mostly written after the composition of the *Missa cuiusvis toni*. Performances of the mass in the sixteenth century probably would have been influenced by these ideas even if the composer did not consciously entertain them as he wrote the composition. There is no way to know whether Ockeghem held the same beliefs about the emotional nature of the modes as any of these writers, but it is likely that he was aware of the associations of modes with emotions. Perhaps he was pragmatic in his assessment—conscious of the sounds of the intervals and their effect on his own mind and those of his listeners rather than simply accepting traditional associations of emotion with modes. In any case, a composition flexible enough to be performed in four modes is fascinating because of the different qualities it takes on as the intervals conform to the diverse structures.

Performance of the *Missa cuiusvis toni*

The notation in this transcription of the *Missa cuiusvis toni* closely follows the original mensural notation that is reproduced in the part-books that accompany the score. In both mensural notation and the transcription, note values are related to a steady beat called the *tactus*. The *tactus* was equated by most theorists with the human pulse, which is readily available even though it is quite variable. It is an indication of a steady tempo, neither slow nor fast, *tempo ordinario*, by which faster or slower tempos may be measured. Just as the human pulse varies, the ordinary tempo may be faster or slower in response to different circumstances of performance. It might reasonably be related to a metronome speed somewhere between 60 and 80.

The *tactus* is indicated in performance by an even down and up motion of the hand. The time duration from one low point of the hand to the next is equated with the note value of the semibreve, the whole-note in modern notation. This equation of *tactus* with the semibreve is indicated by either a circle or a semicircle placed at the beginning of the score. The circle also indicates that the next larger note value, the breve, is subdivided into three semibreves, and the semicircle indicates the subdivision of the breve into two semibreves. "Measure" numbers in the score and parts coincide with the number of breves.

A slash superimposed on the semicircle (or the circle) indicates that the *tactus* is equated with the next larger note value, that is, the breve rather than the semibreve. This is a "duple proportion," and could also be notated by the number 2 or 2/1 placed after the sign. Only the semicircle-with-slash is used in the *Missa cuiusvis toni*. For instance, in the first *Kyrie* signed with a circle, the *tactus* is equal to the semibreve, three of which are included in a breve, and the tempo is moderate. In the *Christe* (semicircle-with-a-slash) the *tactus* is equal to a breve and the notes go by twice as fast. The notation returns to the original relation of *tactus* to semibreve in the second *Kyrie*. Tempo relationships throughout the mass are based on note values and their relation to the *tactus*. This provides a considerable variety in tempos, controlled by *tactus*, proportions, and note values rather than by our modern tempo words.

Mensural notation of tempo was well understood by fifteenth and sixteenth performers; clefless notation such as we find in the *Missa cuiusvis toni* was not, although a performer's solmisation training gave the essential clues needed to solve what seems to us to be a riddle. Solmization is a system that relates pitches to one another through syllables grouped by sixes, or *hexachords*, and which supplements clef notation so effectively that clefs can become redundant. Musicians today usually consider solmization cumbersome and much prefer reading notation in g- and f-clefs, however solmisation clarifies pitch relationships in unexpected ways by revealing melodic imitation at a fourth or fifth as well as at the octave. Through solmisation Ockeghem was able to create a composition performable in four different modes.

---

40. Zarlino, *Istitutioni harmoniche*, Quarta Parte, 322.

The notation of the *Missa cuiusvis toni* in the only printed edition of the 16th century, the *Liber quindecim Missarum a praestantissimis Musicis compositorium*,[41] identifies the location of the finalis of the mode by symbols on the staff rather than by a clef to specify the pitch of notes. The symbols used vary in the print and include dots from which a line rises, signs somewhat like c-clefs and f-clefs, and a circle with a rising line. The performer must decide in which octave to sing each part.

The principal manuscript source, the Chigi Codex[42], notates the modal finalis in similar ways but adds solmisation indications and c-clefs to some sections of the *credo*.[43] The solmization markings identify the Phrygian mode and the clefs specify a pitch on a, transposed up a fourth from e. The Chigi scribe may have used these additional notations to help fix his attention while he copied the manuscript: it is easier to copy music when pitches are clearly in mind rather than just locations on the staff. The Phrygian mode on a places the tessitura of all parts in ranges that are easily sung. Although the modes are associated with specific pitches (d for Dorian, e for Phrygian, f for Lydian, and g for Mixolydian) the essential nature of each mode lies in its intervals rather than in the pitch of its finalis. Singers might use the same pitch for all the modes but vary the intervals as required. Most of the Chigi notation uses only a symbol to indicate the finalis and therefore retains both pitch and modal flexibility.

The mass was called a "catholicon" by Glareanus in his *Dodecachordon*,[44] because of its modal variability not because of its clefless notation. There are other examples of clefless notation in the fifteenth and sixteenth centuries[45], but the *Missa cuiusvis toni* is the only composition that can be performed in different modes, and it is the only large-scale work among them.

Solmization is based on a series of six pitches, the hexachord, invented, according to tradition, by Guido of Arezzo, ca. 1000 a.d., and used by singers throughout the medieval and Renaissance periods. Each hexachord repeats the same relationship of intervals: *ut-re*, tone; *re-mi*, tone; *mi-fa*, semitone; *fa-sol*, tone; and *sol-la*, tone. The pattern is symmetrical, a semitone in the middle with whole steps on either side. *Mi-fa* always indicates a semitone. Three hexachords were the basis of the system: the <u>natural</u>, from c (*ut*) to a (*la*); the <u>hard</u>, from g (*ut*) to e (*la*); and the <u>soft</u>, from f (*ut*) to d (*la*). The hard hexachord contains a hard b (*mi*), b-natural, indicated by the familiar square-shaped natural sign. The soft hexachord uses a soft b (*fa*), b-flat, indicated by a flat sign.

Many melodies move beyond the range of one hexachord, which requires a mutation to the syllables of an adjacent hexachord. A singer must know how to choose between the soft and hard hexachords when leaving the natural, and for this the signature of the part is the best guide. The soft hexachord is chosen whenever there is a b-flat in the key signature and the hard when there is none.

Since the hexachords overlap by two or three notes, there are various points at which a mutation may be made. One can find Renaissance documentation to support different systems, all of which are practical. The illustration below shows the system advocated by Ornithoparcus and John Dowland:

41. Nürnberg: Johannes Petreius, 1539.

42. Biblioteca Vaticana, Chigi C.VIII.234, fol. 96v-106r.

43. In the credo the soprano part has a signature of two flats (each indicating a fa) in measures 94-140 and the alto has a single flat from measure 94 to the end. The tenor has a c-clef from 94 through 137, and the bass has both a c-clef and one flat from 94 to the end. "Measure" numbers correspond both to this and to the Plamenac edition.

44. Basel: Henrichum Petri, 1547, 455.

45. See Joesph Levitan's article "Ockeghem's Clefless Compositions," *The Musical Quarterly*, 23 (1937), 440-64.

The three hexachords were organized into a series of seven called the *gamut*, three octaves and a sixth from G to e'', all the pitches of which were considered to be *musica recta*. Eight pitches are included in the hexachordal octave, from c to b-natural (b-*mi*, or hard b) with b-flat (b-*fa*, or soft b) in addition. Pitches outside of those in the natural, hard, and soft hexachords were considered to be *musica ficta*.

In an ascent through the gamut, mutations are made to *re* of the higher hexachord. From the natural to the hard hexachords (a fifth apart), the singer moves from *sol* to *re* (to replace *la*), and from the hard to the natural hexachords (a fourth apart), *fa* to *re* (to replace *sol*). In descent, mutations are made to *la* of the lower hexachord. Therefore, from the hard to the natural hexachord the singer descends from *mi* to *la* (to replace *re*), and from the natural to the hard, *fa* to *la* (to replace *mi*). This puts the singer in the lower part of the new hexachord in ascent (without using *ut*) and in the upper part of the new hexachord in descent. The mutations between natural and soft hexachords are similar, with the difference that the soft hexachord is a fourth higher than the natural, and the natural a fifth higher than the soft.

Solmisation syllables identify the characteristic intervals of each mode. The most significant intervals of any mode are the fifth from the finalis up to the confinalis and the fourth from the confinalis up to the octave of the finalis. *Re-la* identifies the first species of fifth (Dorian), *mi-mi* the second species (Phrygian), *fa-fa* the third (Lydian) and *ut-sol* the fourth (Mixolydian). *Re-sol* identifies the first species of fourth, *mi-la* the second, and *ut-fa* the third. The Mixolydian mode reuses *re-sol* to complete its range and as a result some theorists gave the mode secondary status.

Two additional modes, Æolian and Ionian, were reluctantly added to the canon only in the sixteenth century because their component fifths and fourths are all reused intervals of other modes. The Æolian fifth is *re-la* (as is the Dorian), the fourth is *mi-la* (as is the Phrygian), and the Ionian intervals are *ut-sol* (Mixolydian) and *ut-fa* (Lydian). The *Missa cuiusvis toni* was not conceived with them in mind.

The relation of solmization and notation is illustrated in Example 2 (p. 25). Line 1 has a mode-sign that indicates the finalis of the mode, three dots from which a curved line ascends, on the second line of the staff, followed by fifths and fourths solmized in the Dorian mode. After the first double bar on line 1, solmization flats serve as a "key signature," to indicate where *fas* will be sung. The *fas* are a fifth apart as are the hexachords in which they are found. The required hexachords are not specified and may be on different pitches, for instance a natural hexachord above a soft hexachord, or a hard hexachord above a natural. After the second double bar on line one, a g-clef locates the Dorian intervals on specific pitches. If the Dorian mode is written as a scale, the semitones are found between steps 2 and 3 and 6 and 7, as shown by line 2 of Example 2.

Lines 3 through 8 show the intervals and solmizations of the other authentic modes, and lines 9 and 10 show those of the plagal modes. Signature flats and sharps in clefless notation have quite a different meaning than those in clef notation. For each mode the solmisation signature changes, placed lower on the staff as the finalis rises from d to e (Phrygian), and e to f (Lydian). The Mixolydian solmization signature places a sharp and a flat a fifth apart on the staff, to show where *mi* and *fa* are sung. The hexachords are therefore a fourth apart instead of a fifth, with the natural placed above the hard, or the soft placed above the natural.

Neither the sign that identifies a modal finalis or a solmization signature designates a unique pitch on the staff. The modal finalis or signature flats (*fas*) and sharps (*mis*) show a combination of hexachords, that is, pitches that are relative to one another. A singer is free to choose any suitable pitch. Only if an instrument were included in the ensemble would absolute pitch be necessary.

In Examples 3 through 10, solmization and mutations are indicated below the staves. Mutation is shown by slashes (/) between syllables in different hexachords. Phrases may have an influence on solmization, for instance the phrase that ends the first line of the soprano part in Example 3 (p. 26) remains in the upper hexachord (a fifth higher than the lower), even though it could be sung as *sol* in the new hexachord, to which a mutation must be made after the two tempora rest.

When there are large skips in a line, a mutation should include the immediately adjacent hexachord, otherwise a disjunction, or mental omission of the intervening intervals would occur. An octave between two cs is not solmized with the same syllable, for instance *ut-ut,* or *fa-fa,* because that would omit the intervening hexachord, and the intermediate pitches would not be understood from the solmization. The octave should be sung *ut-fa* or *ut-sol,* to identify b-*mi* or b-*fa* in the intervening pitches, even though they are not sung.

Solmisation helps to identify intervals that require an alteration of pitch by the singer. When *mi* in one hexachord is closely followed by *fa* in another, or *fa* by *mi,* the melodic interval between them is an augmented fourth or a diminished fifth. Theorists tell us that these intervals were considered difficult to sing, and discordant to the ear, and that they were tolerated only in special circumstances. Linear augmented fourths and diminished fifths were usually corrected by the alteration of *mi* to *fa,* which lowers the pitch a semitone with a flat. As we shall see, certain passages in the mass are much more simply resolved by the addition of a sharp or a natural, which raises *fa* by a semitone to *mi.* Karol Berger cites three theorists, Johannes Hothby (fl.1567-87), Bonaventura da Brescia (1497), and Lanfranco (1533) who allow the correction of the linear conflict of *mi contra fa* by a sharp rather than by a flat.[46]

A melodic *mi contra fa,* particularly if it is not created by a direct leap, may be resolved by a continuation of the melody by one semitone, either immediately or delayed by a few intervening notes. If the interval is an augmented fourth from f-*fa* up to b-*mi,* b-natural, a further melodic semitone to c-*fa* satisfies the ear, and if it is from b-*mi* down to f-*fa,* subsequent movement to e-*mi* provides a resolution. A diminished fifth from f-*fa* down to b-*mi* is resolved by a semitone to c-*fa,* and a diminished fifth from b-*mi* up to f-*fa* is resolved by e-*mi.*[47] Another circumstance in which a melodic tritone or diminished fifth can be left uncorrected is when the notes of the interval are separated by a rest.[48] Musicians today should keep in mind that singers read their music from part books rather than from scores and therefore the melodic line was initially the only clue from which to gauge the need for alteration. Linear tritones and diminished fifths are fairly easy to spot, even at first sight.

The first stage of solmisation might be considered to be the singer's recognition of melodic intervals together with the alteration of any melodic tritones or diminished fifths. A second stage would consider

46. Berger, 81.
47. Berger, 76 and 79.
48. Berger, 76.

whether simultaneous intervals or harmonies need to be altered. Harmonies requiring correction can be considered in two categories, harmonic clashes and cadential progressions.

Harmonic tritones and diminished fifths, also recognized by the syllables *mi contra fa*, were as little tolerated as melodic, however not all these intervals are avoidable. Musicians were obliged to consider when and where *mi contra fa* might become acceptable, both in linear and harmonic intervals. Usually singers were allowed to add only one flat beyond the key signature to avoid *mi contra fa*.[49] This requires a certain tolerance for the tritone, and makes chains of flats in order to correct successive conflicts impossible. This limit is derived from the instructions of several theorists, but most directly reflects the views of Johannes Tinctoris in his *Liber de natura et proprietate tonorum in Opera theoretica* of 1476, almost contemporary with the *Missa cuiusvis toni*.

In the late fifteenth and sixteenth centuries, harmonic tritones and diminished fifths were usually altered by the introduction of a flat, as were their linear counterparts. An important difference is evident in the practice before roughly 1470. Berger states "no theoretical evidence presented here to support my claim that *mi* against *fa* is normally corrected by means of a flat dates from before the 1470s. Indeed the evidence from before that time points to a different conclusion: theorists of the fourteenth and earlier fifteenth centuries correct *mi* against *fa* by both flats and sharps."[50] Ockeghem would have been about sixty years old in 1470 and it is likely the the *Missa cuiusvis toni* would have been conceived and interpreted according to the rules of the early fifteenth century. The evidence of the work itself, as we shall see, makes the use of sharps as likely as flats to correct harmonic conflicts of *mi contra fa*.

If a tritone or diminished fifth must be tolerated when both linear and harmonic conflicts occur, preference must be given to a correction of the harmonic over the linear interval.[51] If a harmonic dissonance is unavoidable, the melodic progression to and from it should be by the closest possible intervals.[52]

Cadences are recognized as instances where sharps are regularly used to provide the desired resolutions, and it is rare that a flat is introduced to establish a proper cadence. Cadences may be briefly described as two-part contrapuntal progressions to either a unison or an octave—perfect consonances suitable as resting places to 15th- and 16th-century musicians. A cadential progression approaches the unison or octave by the closest melodic intervals, a tone in one part and a semitone in the other. This means that the unison must be preceded by a minor third and the octave by a major sixth, in order for a listener to recognize it as a cadence. Since diatonic intervals in all the modes do not produce these cadential progressions, the performer must alter them if a cadence is appropriate and desirable. This usually means that the upper voice must be raised a semitone, by the introduction of a sharp, *mi*, on the penultimate note of a cadential resolution.

Cadences are not made solely by two-voiced harmonic progressions although two voices are the essential framework. Other voices of the composition must participate with intervals that do not contradict the cadence, it must take place in a suitable metrical position, and the text must come to a grammatical conclusion simultaneously with the music. Performers influence the musical structure either by altering the pitch or leaving notes unchanged at cadential intervals, in order to avoid cadences where there is no grammatical conclusion.[53]

These general principles may be illustrated by the beginning of the Sanctus of the *Missa cuiusvis toni*. Example 3 (p. 26) presents the original notation of the singers' parts solmized in the Phrygian mode, cor-

---

49. Karol Berger states: "pieces in which all internal accidentals were introduced in order to avoid melodic and vertical non-harmonic intervals would use at most one more flat than the number of flats in the key signature of the voice with the largest number of flats in the signature." *Musica ficta*, 121.

50. Berger, 117.

51. Berger, 119.

52. Berger, 95-107.

53. Houle, *Doulce memoire: a study in performance practice*, Bloomington: Indiana University Press, 1990, 8-10.

responding to measures 1 through 16 of the score in Example 4 (page 27), with the Phrygian mode transposed to a. The syllable sung on the first note depends on the subsequent direction of the line, so that for a rising line the first note should use a syllable low in a hexachord, and a descending line should use a syllable high in a hexachord. If we use the solmization of the Phrygian mode proposed in line 3 of Example 2, *mi* is the first syllable of both soprano and tenor parts and *la* is the first syllable for alto and bass.

Only one linear *mi contra fa* is found in this excerpt, a diminished fourth in the tenor part on line 7 of Example 3, where it is marked by a bracket between *mi* and *fa*, with two asterisks placed by the second syllable. A singer would ordinarily sing the *mi* a semitone lower as *fa* to correct the interval. However, when this correction is sung with the other parts, it will be heard to cause another *mi contra fa*, a diminished octave with the bass. This is quickly seen when the parts are in score (Example 4, measure 5), but would have become apparent to singers with part books only in performance. A correction of the bass *mi* to *fa* would bring a linear tritone in the bass part with the preceding a (although it is solmized *la*), and if this were corrected in turn it would cause a harmonic diminished fifth against the alto e-natural, *mi*, the first note in measure 5. This chain of corrections would violate the general rule to limit additional corrective flats to one beyond the key signature. Corrections would continue still further, since the alto e-flat would require linear a-flats before and after it in order to avoid linear tritones. It would take a great deal of time and effort to make so many trials and corrections. Notes far in advance of the trouble spot would have to be altered as well as subsequent notes. This is an unlikely solution to the problem.

There is also a harmonic augmented fourth in this passage that will need correction, a *mi contra fa* between the tenor and alto on the first notes of measure 5, marked in Example 3 with single asterisks. With the score in hand and in light of the discussion above, it is clear that if this interval is altered with an e-flat, the same chain reaction will be started. However, if the *fa* were raised a semitone by a sharp the tritone would be avoided and no chain would result. We might consider whether the same alteration would satisfy the problem of the linear *mi contra fa* between the fourth and sixth notes of the tenor in measure 5. With score in hand, we can see that if the second *fa* in the tenor in measure 5 is sung *mi* it will conflict with *fa* in both alto and bass. On further investigation, however, we see that the resolution of this new tritone and diminished fifth is very smooth, the *fa* descends a third and the *mi* ascends a semitone. Tinctoris would tolerate the harmonic tritone produced by the b-*mi* at the end of measure 5 because of the smooth voice leading surrounding the interval.[54] The problems of this passage may therefore be resolved by the addition of two raised semitones, b-naturals, with a resulting diminished fifth dissonance resolved by smooth voice leading. The simplicity of this solution is a practical advantage.

Cadential alterations of pitch depend as much on the grammar of the text as on the intervals of the cadential voices. The first grammatical unit is complete on the seventh measure of the Sanctus (see p. 53 for the text setting) where *Sanctus* gives way to *Dominus Deus*. An octave a is approached by step in the alto and bass, and a fifth is approached by step between the tenor and bass. With the alteration of the minor sixth interval by a c-*mi* (c-sharp) before the octave to make a major sixth, it will be heard as a cadence.

The next cadence may be produced on the last semibreve of measure 11 where soprano and tenor move by step to an octave, and a c-sharp will create a minor third that resolves to a unison. This interval might be cadential but it is contradicted by its weak rhythmic position, the textual overlap with the next phrase, and by the bass which moves to b-flat, a third below the cadential d. It is therefore ambiguous, weak at best, and easily avoided if the c in the tenor remains natural. The cadence at measure 15 is similarly weakened by the counterpoint in the bass and no textual completion. Cadential inflections are consequentially optional in measures 11 and 14. The score has included the c-sharp in measure 14, but not that in 11. The exerpt ends on a, the modal finalis, in measure 16, but without a firm cadential resolution.

Examples 5 and 6 (pp. 28 and 29) present the same excerpt with Mixolydian solmization. There are no linear conflicts of *mi contra fa* to be resolved, but there are two harmonic diminished fifths, the first

---

54. Berger, 95-6.

between soprano (*fa*) and tenor (*mi*) in measure 7, and the other among alto (*fa*), bass, and soprano (both *mi*) in measure 8. If the *mi*s in measure 8 are made *fa*s, the bass will move by a linear tritone to e *mi* in measure 9, and if this e is flatted, it will conflict with an octave e natural in the tenor, and so begins a chain of corrections that will continue for two more measures. The simpler solution here is to use a sharp on f-*fa* in the alto, and this suggests that f-*mi* in the soprano in measure 7 might be used as well.

Modal context is related to the use of altered degrees, according to Jacques de Liège, whose early fourteenth-century treatise already reflects the standard doctrine of the period.[55] In the Mixolydian, the linear b-flat is avoided because it transforms the mode into the Dorian, but f-sharp does not disrupt the identity of the mode, provided that it is introduced as a cadential leading tone. This makes the use of f-sharp more common in the Mixolydian because of cadences to the finalis and melodic patterns that center around g. In the Mixolydian *Missa cuiusvis toni*, this modal tolerance of f-sharp suggests solutions to difficult passages where *mi contra fa* cannot easily be resolved by the use of b-flat.

No cadential alterations are required in Examples 5 and 6, since the cadences to the fourth degree of the mode fall on c.

Examples 7 and 8 (pp. 30 and 31) show solmization in Lydian and offer two possible interpretations. The first, "with b-*mi*," demonstrates what solmization would be if the hard hexachord were assumed throughout. It is evident that the *mi contra fa* between the modal finalis and the fourth tone of the mode (an augmented fourth) is highly obtrusive and requires a number of alterations in order to avoid linear tritones. Of thirty-nine b pitches in this example, thirty-six must be altered to b-*fa* to avoid *mi contra fa*, and only three, two in the soprano in measure 2 and one in the tenor, measure 5, can be sung as b-*mi*, because of linear resolutions by the addition of one semitone, *mi* to *fa*. If b-flat is included in the signature in order to recognize the use of the soft hexachord in the Lydian mode, all three of these optional b-naturals will be b-flats, and alteration of e-naturals to e-*fa* will be allowed. Discussions of the Lydian mode usually specify that the fifth and sixth modes use the soft hexachord: Ornithoparchus, in John Dowland's translation states "All the *Tones* runne under the scale of b-*dure*, excepting the fift and the sixt."[56] Karol Berger sums up theorists' views on the use of b-*fa* in these modes: "In their various ways, theorists reflect the tension between the theoretical tradition according to which the intervallic species proper to the untransposed modes 5 and 6 use the square b and the practical reality in which most pieces in these modes are notated with a flat b signature."[57]

The Lydian mode on f with one flat in the signature becomes a different set of intervals, identical to Glareanus's Ionian. Apparently this change did not dissuade musicians from the regular use of a b-flat, and for good reason, as we can see when almost all the b-*mi*s in the Lydian mode must be altered to avoid nonharmonic intervals anyway. The b-flat Lydian mode was unique in its intervals, at least before the recognition of the Ionian mode, even if the intervals differed from those of the b-natural Lydian.

The use of a b-flat signature does more than eliminate many of the conflicts of *mi contra fa*, it becomes "the flat that may be exceeded by one" in order to correct additional tritone dissonances. In measure 2 of the soprano part, b-*mi* is a linear tritone with the first note, f-*fa*, the finalis. However b-*mi* ascends to c-*fa*, to resolve the tritone to the fifth from f-*fa*. This is an adequate resolution and makes alteration of the b-*mi* unnecessary.[58] If a b-flat signature were present, a linear tritone would occur between b-*fa* and e-*mi* in measure 2 of the alto part, with the same resolution by voice leading that we have seen in the soprano part in the absence of the b-flat signature. Another linear tritone is created in measure 14 in the

55. Berger, 82-3.

56. Ornithoparchus/Dowland, *A Compendium of Musical Practice*, ed. by Gustave Reese and Steven Ledbetter. New York: Dover Publications, Inc., 1973, 135.

57. Berger, 60.

58. Berger, 73-5.

bass that does require alteration of e-*mi* to *fa*. All the other tritones that need resolution are harmonic. In measure 6 of the alto part, the signature b-flat is in harmonic conflict with e-*mi* in the tenor which might be altered to e-*fa*, or left e-*mi* since it resolves by semitone to f. The same conflict is resolved by e-*fa* between the tenor and bass in measure 9, requiring e in the soprano, an octave above the bass, to become e-*fa*. The e-*fas* in measures 11, 12, 13, and 15 are necessary to correct harmonic conflicts.

Cadences on the fourth tone of the mode in Examples 7 and 8 must fall on b-*fa*. Ockeghem's emphasis on the fourth degree of the mode as a frequent cadential point requires b-flat in order to avoid a tritone between it and the finalis. This may have been done to confirm the regular use of the soft hexachord for the Lydian mode in the singer's mind. Cadences in measures 6/7, 11, and 14/15 do not require alteration of the written pitches.

The score of the Lydian version of the mass does not use a b-flat signature. This clarifies the theoretical b-*mi* version of the Lydian to the eye of the analyst and exposes the few b-*mis* that are not required to be altered by harmonic or linear conflicts. However, e-*mi* is treated as an alterable degree as if b-*fa* were in the signature.

Examples 9 and 10 (pp. 32 and 33) show solmization in the Dorian mode on g, transposed up a fourth with a signature of b-flat. E-flat becomes the additional flat permitted to resolve conflicts of *mi contra fa*. Line 1 of the soprano part has two strong conflicts of *mi contra fa* outlined between the third and sixth tones of the mode, these are the highest notes of the phrase. To correct the soprano by changing the high e-*mis* to *fas* results in a diminished fifth between the soprano (e-flat) and alto (a) on the last note of measure 3. This seems to need correction, but would require an unacceptable second flat beyond the signature, a-flat. However the rhythmic position of this clash allows a dissonance resolved by step-wise progression. The other tritones outlined by brackets in the soprano are resolved by flats that alter *mis* to *fas* that do not in turn cause any other non-harmonic intervals. Linear tritones in the other three voices are all resolved with no harmonic conflicts by flats on the *mis* indicated by brackets.

The harmonic conflicts marked with single asterisks in Examples 9 and 10 are similarly resolved by flats in every instance. Some of these are motivated by a primary correction in one voice with which a second voice must agree, but only one flat beyond the signature is involved.

In the Dorian mode, the fourth degree, on which so many cadences fall, requires a raised third tone of the mode, b-natural. A cadence is negated by a b-*mi* at the end of measure 6 that creates a tritone with the tenor f-*fa*. Since both the tenor and alto move up by step, the resolution of the tritone is not as smooth as it would be if the tenor were to resolve by motion down a step. A potential cadence at the last semibreve of measure 11 would not create this harmonic dissonance, but the text and rhythm offer little reason for a cadence. In measures 14-15, the cadence is weakened by the bass line, but the score alters the cadential interval in order to emphasize it in relation to the weaker point of arrival in measure 11.

These are the principal conflicts to be resolved so that one is now prepared to study the basic technique of singing the *Missa cuiusvis toni*.

The Mass in the Phrygian Mode

The problems of solmization in the Phrygian mode are rather few and alterations of discords are readily made, although some passages can be puzzling. Cadences to the fourth degree of the mode are frequent and in this edition these these fall on d, a pitch that requires c-sharp for its harmonic cadential progression. In the *Kyrie* the only accidental required is the cadential c-sharp at the end of measure 26. A new phrase of the text begins at measure 27, coupled with a textural change from two to three voices that seems sufficient justification for a cadence. In measure 5/6 of the *Gloria* there is a cadence to c, the third degree of the mode, and there is a potential cadence to the fourth degree in measure 70 that might require a c-sharp. This would set off the text phrase *Jesu Christe*, but it is also possible that the flow of the music might be smoother without this cadential alteration.

There are no linear tritones or diminished fifths in the *Credo* but ten alterations of pitch are needed to avoid harmonic conflicts of *mi contra fa*, six of which are tritones. These are altered by flats in measures 3, 19, 106, and 121 and by sharps in measures 182 and 183. Four harmonic diminished fifths are altered by sharps in measures 148, 171, 172, and 173, two are resolved by voice leading in measures 25 and 88, and two more occur in normal positions for dissonances in measures 29 and 91. Cadences to the fourth degree of the mode account for all the potential c-sharps in the *Credo*. At measure 12, there is an old-fashioned 7-6-8 cadential melodic phrase in the bass that requires both c-sharp and b-natural, and both of these alterations are required again in measure 119. Cadences at measures 55/56, 114/115, and 154/155 require only c-sharps. A cadence in measure 173/174, the end of a major section of the *Credo*, is negated by a doubled leading tone.

The first section of the *Sanctus* has been discussed above, and an account made of the linear and harmonic tritones altered by sharps in measure 5 and the cadences to d in measures 6/7 and 14/15. In the following *Pleni* section, harmonic tritones are altered by flats in measures 30 and 31, harmonic diminished fifths are altered by flats in measures 20 and 22, and by b-naturals in measures 24, 28, and 29. A linear tritone requires a flat in measure 31. In the *Osanna*, b-naturals alter harmonic diminished fifths in measures 28 and 36, and a harmonic tritone in measure 34; there are two cadences with c-sharps (16/17, and 32/33). There is one cadential alteration in the *Benedictus* at measure 9, a c-sharp. In the *Qui venit*, e-flats alter the two harmonic diminished fifths in measures 12 and 23, and another is resolved by voice leading in measure 9/10. Two cadences to a require to c-sharps in measures 6 and 29/30.

In the *Agnus dei*, all the *mi contra fa* conflicts are resolved by raised semitones; five harmonic tritones in measures 10, 11, 14, 19, and 35, and three harmonic diminished fifths in measures 15, 20, and 46. There are three cadences to d with c-sharps in measures 3/4, 11/12, and 28/29.

This totals thirty-one *mi contra fa* conflicts. Harmonic tritones are resolved by flats in six instances and by sharps in nine, harmonic diminished fifths by flats in two instances and by sharps in twelve. There are only two linear tritones, one corrected by a flat and one by a sharp, and there are no linear diminished fifths. This is a very small number of alterations, a fact that reinforces the hypothesis that the mass was composed with the Phrygian mode in mind.

The Mass in the Mixolydian Mode

The first harmonic diminished fifth in the *Kyrie* is in measure 14 of the *Christe*, between the tenor and alto. It is both approached and resolved by semitones that make it unnecessary to alter the interval.[59] A change to b-*fa* would have caused a subsequent unavoidable linear tritone, and a change to f-*mi* would require the ear to disregard some curious cross relations of f-sharp and c-natural. An f-*mi* in the alto in measure 30 (*Kyrie* II) resolves a harmonic tritone with the soprano and a diminished fifth with the tenor where b-flats would have brought additional tritones.

In the Mixolydian mode, cadences to the modal finalis require an f-*mi*, and cadences to the fourth degree of the mode, c, require no alteration. Cadences to the finalis are less frequent than those to the fourth degree and therefore the number of cadential alterations in the Mixolydian is reduced from those in the Phrygian mode. There are only two cadences in the *Kyrie*, both to the finalis.

Counterpoints in the Mixolydian mode make linear conflicts of *mi contra fa* as rare as in the Phrygian mode. There are only three in the *Gloria*, the first of which should not be altered. This is at measure 14 in the bass, where a b-*fa* (which avoids harmonic diminished fifths with both soprano and tenor) precedes an

---

59. Berger, 93.

e-*mi*. The bass must alter its b-natural because the soprano f-*fa* precedes the bass b-*mi*. The linear diminished fifth is excused because of the intervening rest.[60] The second linear conflict is in the alto in measure 17 and resolved by raising f-*fa* to f-*mi*. The third is in measure 83 in the soprano where correction by b-*fa* brings an harmonic diminished fifth with e-*mi* in the alto. This is resolved by semitone with no alteration of e-*mi*, however, b-natural in the tenor must be altered twice as a consequence and the second e-*mi* in the alto must be changed to e-*fa*.

There are four harmonic tritones in the *Gloria*, three of these are resolved by sharps (measures 5, 9, and 41), and one by a flat (measure 28). Four harmonic diminished fifths are altered by sharps (measures 4, 6, 21, and 68), one by a flat (measure 14) and one is resolved by voice leading (measure 12). A cadence to the fifth degree, d, in the third measure of the *Gloria*, requires a c-sharp, otherwise the cadential alterations are all f-*mi*s at cadences to the finalis (measures 10/11, 30/31, 49/50, and 85/86).

The greater number of harmonic conflicts of *mi contra fa* in the *Credo* are diminished fifths, thirteen of which are altered by sharps (measures 25, 64, 98, 126, 145, 146, 148, 149, 159, 170/171, 179, and 180). One is resolved by a flat (measure 162), three are resolved by voice leading (measures 35/36, 72, 100/101) and one by recognizing that the conflict is in a normal position for dissonance (measure 161). Harmonic tritones are resolved by a sharp in measure 140 and by a flat in measure 182; linear tritones by a sharp in measure 21 and by a flat in measure 53/54. Five cadences to the modal finalis require sharps in measures 7/8, 21/22, 43/44, 91/92, and 123/124; a cadence to the sixth degree, e, in measure 25/26 requires that the diminished fifth b to f be altered to a perfect fifth, b to f-sharp, before the resolution to e. At the end of the *Credo*, the final cadence to the modal finalis cannot be made with an f-*mi* because of a conflicting f-*fa* in the tenor. Counterpoint precludes proper final cadences in both Mixolydian and Dorian modes, but cadences in Phrygian and Lydian occur without pitch alterations.

There are nine harmonic diminished fifths in the *Sanctus*, five of which are altered by sharps (measures 7, 8, 23 of the *Osanna*, 12 and 27 of the *Qui venit*), two by position (measures 27 and 28 of the *Sanctus*), and two by voice leading (measures 5 and 17/18 of the *Qui venit*). Two linear tritones require sharps in measures 23 and 24 of the *Sanctus*. Four cadences to the modal finalis are altered with f-sharps (measures 25/26 of the *Sanctus*; 9/10 and 40/41 of the *Osanna*; and 12 of the *Benedictus*). A cadence to the sixth degree of the mode, e, in measure 15/16 of the *Qui venit* makes both f-sharp and d-sharp necessary.

Linear tritones in the *Agnus* are resolved by b-*fa* in measures 7 and 46/47 and by voice leading in 7/8. Harmonic diminished fifths are resolved by flats in measures 10 and 46, by a sharp in measure 39, and by position in measure 14. Four cadences to g require f-sharps in measures 11/12, 15/16, 22/23, and 48/49.

The Mass in the Lydian Mode

The Lydian version of the *Missa cuiusvis toni* offers many linear tritones that are resolved by a semitone expansion to fifths. These rise from b-flat through e-natural to f, or occasionally from f through b-natural to c. Possibly Ockeghem was teaching his singers every way to interpret this interval. When the tritone is followed by an additional semitone, no alteration of the discord is necessary even if the additional semitone is delayed by one or several notes. If the tritone does not rise through this semitone, the notes b-*mi* or e-*mi* should be altered to *fa*. There may occasionally be a harmonic conflict with b-*mi*, e-*mi*, b-*fa*, or e-*fa* that must be heard in order to make a proper adjustment. The pedagogic value of the Lydian mass is such that after singing it, one knows how to perform analogous melodic passages in any repertory.

The notation of this edition does not use a b-flat signature, so that our attention is focussed on the b-naturals that remain unchanged by linear or harmonic necessity. Of 722 b pitches in the Lydian mass, 664 are altered to b-flat (92%), and 58 remain b-natural (8%). B-flat is so frequently required that it seems

---

60. Berger, 76.

pedantic not to place it in the signature, but a b-flat signature would obscure the few exceptional b-naturals, and the rather interesting 8% would be lost to the ear. However, it is possible that those exceptional b-naturals were never intended to stand unaltered.

Singing from a score or parts which lack a b-flat signature for the Lydian mode requires care and calculation that would not be necessary were the signature included. All cadences on the fourth degree must take place on b-flat to avoid the structural tritone relationship of the fourth and first degree of the mode, regardless of whether there is an immediate linear or harmonic interval to alert the singer to use b-*fa*,

If there were a b-flat signature, e-flat (e-*fa*) would be available to correct additional intervallic conflicts. This edition treats e-flat as an available alteration even though b-flat is not in the signature. The only sharps required in the Lydian mode are those needed at cadences to d, the sixth tone of the mode, and b-naturals that approach c cadences should be regarded as equivalent to sharped notes in the context of the Lydian mass.

In the *Kyrie*, linear tritones require flats in measures 2/3, 5, 6, 12/13, 27, 28, and 29, and linear tritones with naturals are resolved by voice leading in measures 1 and 28. Linear diminished fifths require flats in measures 21, 23/24, 25, and 29/30; a linear diminished fifth is resolved by voice leading in measure 1. One harmonic tritone in measure 17 requires a flat, and harmonic diminished fifths require flats in measures 5, 6, 13, 19, 26, and 31.

In the *Gloria*, linear tritones are resolved by flats in measures 9, 10, 12, 15, 17, 18, 19/20, 22, 24, 27, 28/29, 30, 46/47, 47/48, 52, 55, 56, 58, 59, 63, 64/65, 66/68, 68/69, 78/79, 81/82, and 84. Linear tritones with b-naturals are resolved by voice leading in measures 1, 9, 11, 25, and 82/83. Linear diminished fifths are corrected by flats in measures 9, 15, 19, 21/22, 24, 27, 29, 35/36, 39/40, 71, 75, 76, and 84/85; and one linear diminished fifth in measure 72 is resolved through voice leading. Harmonic tritones in measures 5, 20, 28, 40, 56, and 70 require flats, and diminished fifths in measures 15, 20, 21, 25, 27, 28, 42, 56, 65, 70, 77, 78, 81, and 82 require flats. Harmonic diminished fifths in measures 4/5, 26/27, and 72 are resolved by voice leading. Only one cadence, in measures 5/6, needs an altered pitch, in this case a b-*fa* to provide a Phrygian cadence on a, the third degree of the mode. Cadences to the finalis do not need an accidental, and those to the fifth degree use b-natural, which is ambiguous as an accidental.

In the *Credo* linear tritones require flats in measures 1-3, 5, 7, 8/9, 10, 14, 16, 17, 18, 19/20, 23, 29/30, 32/33, 36-39 ,48/49, 51, 52, 56/57, 60/61, 68/69, 71-73, 75/76, 79, 80/81, 83, 84/85, 90, 91/92, 94-96, 97, 106, 107/108, 113/114, 118, 121/122, 123/124, 134/135, 136, 139, 151/152, 158-160, 161/162, 163/164, 173, 179/180, 182, 183/184, and 186/187. Linear tritones are resolved by voice leading, without alteration, in measures 166/167, 175/176, and 179. Linear diminished fifths are much fewer, and are resolved by flats in measures 5/6, 11, 18, 32, 41/42, 75, 78, 80 82, 82/83, 88/89, 91, 138/139, 142, 165/166, 168/169, 173/174, 186, and 187. One is resolved by voice leading in measures 134/135. Two harmonic tritones require flats in measures 19 and 164, and one is resolved by voice leading in measure 101. Harmonic diminished fifths are resolved by flats in measures 4-6, 17, 30, 31, 45, 65, 67, 80, 99, 103, 107, 108, 115, 122, 125, 135, 136, 137, 138, 140, 161, 162, 168, 171, 172, 182, and 185. One is resolved by voice leading in measures 143/144. Cadences to the sixth degree of the mode, d (measures 25/26), and the fifth, c (measures 180/181) require alterations of pitch.

In the *Sanctus* linear tritones require flats in measures 3 4, 6, 9, 10, 12, 13, 14, 18, 19/20, 22, 23/24, 25, 26, 27, 31, and 32; voice leading resolves one linear tritone in measures 1/2. Linear diminished fifths require flats in measures 14, 22, 25, 26/27, 29/30, and 32. One harmonic tritone in measure 30 needs a flat, one harmonic diminished fifth in measure 4 is resolved by voice leading. Flats to resolve diminished fifths are required in measures 6, 7, 8, 1, 18, 20, 21, 25, 32, and 33. In the *Osanna*, linear tritones require flats in measures 1/2, 6, 14-17, 20/21, 30/31, 31/32, 35/36, and 39/40. A linear diminished fifth is resolved by voice leading in measures 10/11. Harmonic tritones are resolved with flats in measures 10, 24, and 35; harmonic diminished fifths are resolved with flats in measures 1, 3, 4, 6, 8, 10, 13, 18, 25, 26, 27, 28, 30,

31, 36, 37, and 38. In the brief two-part *Benedictus*, flats resolve linear tritones in measures 1/2, 5, 6, 6/7, and 11; one is resolved by voice leading in measures 2/4; and one linear diminished fifth is altered by a flat in measure 3. In the *Qui venit* linear tritones are flatted in measures 2/3, 3/4, 5, 8, 11/12, 21/22, 24/25, 27, and 28. A linear tritone in the bass in measures 27/28 is resolved by voice leading. Altered linear diminished fifths are found in measures 5/6, 8/9, 26/27, and 29/30. Harmonic diminished fifths are altered by flats in measures 13, 17, 18, 20, 25, and 26. One cadence in measures 15/16 to the sixth degree of the mode, d, requires a c-sharp.

In the *Agnus dei*, one linear tritone has neither a good resolution by voice leading nor an alteration, in the tenor part in measures 47/48 of *Agnus* II. Since a complicated web of flats ensues from making corrections, such as a-flats beyond the limit of permissable alterations, the tritone has been left unchanged in this edition. Other linear tritones are altered by flats in measures 1, 2, 4, 6, 9/10, 13, 14/15, 24/25, 27, 32, 41/442, and 43. One linear tritone is resolved by voice leading in measures 37/38. Linear diminished fifths are altered in measures 3, 4, 12/13, 13, 17/18, 24/25, and 42/43. Harmonic diminished fifths are flatted in measures 2, 5, 6, 7, 19, 22, 30, 34, 37, 40, 43, 44, 45, and 46.

In the Lydian mass there are so many required alterations that occasionally the melodic consistency of a line is threatened when an alteration of pitch is not required. It is irresistable to restore the characteristic smoothness of Ockeghem's melody lines in such an instance, even though there may be no specific linear or harmonic reason to justify an alteration. An example can be found in measure 14 of the *Credo* where an additional b-natural seems advisable. More instances of alteration for the sake of melodic consistency will be seen in the Dorian version.

The Mass in the Dorian Mode

In the Dorian *Kyrie* we see more linear conflicts of *mi contra fa* than in the *Kyries* of the other modes. The soprano part frequently turns on the third and sixth degrees, which in the Dorian are *fa* and *mi*. Adjustments of these conflicts bring about secondary tritones, diminished fifths, octaves, and augmented octaves and not all of them can be corrected. Difficult choices are asked of the performer, such as whether to tolerate primary or secondary clashes when a dissonance cannot be entirely avoided. Theorists advise that avoidance of an harmonic tritone is preferable if a choice must be made between the correction of either a linear or harmonic tritone. The best choice is not always so clear from the musical context. Whatever choice the performer makes, unresolved dissonant conflicts must be tolerated in the Dorian mass.

Every measure of the first *Kyrie* requires one or more e-*fas* to avoid tritones, most of which are linear. A linear tritone requires an a-*fa* in measure 3 (alto), and harmonic conflict requires an a-*fa* in measure 4 (tenor), and again in measure 5 (soprano). These alterations break the rule against the introduction of more than one flat beyond the signature, but seem musically preferable because unresolved tritones in measures 3 and 6 and a diminished fifth in measure 4 are harsh and obvious. Linear tritones require e-*fas* in measures 9-11, 15, 17, 21, 25, 30/31, and 32. In measure 5 (alto, fourth minim) a diminished fifth against the soprano is resolved by semitone melodic progressions in both voices. Two cadences to the modal finalis require f-*mis* (measures 7 and 31/32), and three to the fourth degree require b-*mis* (measures 19, 27, and 29).

Ockeghem's cadential emphasis on the fourth degree of the mode, c in this edition of the Dorian mass, results in a number of passages where counterpoints revolve around the fifth between c and g, particularly in the soprano and tenor parts. Leeman Perkins has pointed out that by the consistent use of e-*fa*, with the occasional additional alteration of a to a-*fa*, this fifth becomes the Dorian fifth, *re-la*, with its frequently encountered semitone one note beyond the fifth.[61] There are a number of passages in the *Gloria* and *Credo* where such alterations would present the Dorian fifth on both g and c, for instance measures 18-26 and 56-

---

61. Private correspondence, May 22, 1990.

59 in the *Gloria*; and measures 12-20, 67-87, 109-139, and 160-174 in the *Credo*. There is much to be said for alterations based on this insightful analytical perception which result in smooth linear and harmonic intervals as well as the rhyming Dorian fifths.

Despite these advantages, which are clear from reading the score, it is difficult to see how performers would know from their parts when to introduce the alterations for this modal consistency. The guiding principle of alterations suggested in this edition is to adjust discordant intervals, first linear then harmonic, in the simplest way possible. In the passages cited above, this produces a commixture of the Mixolydian fifth on c with the Dorian fifth on g by the alteration b-*fa* to b-*mi* rather than e-*mi* to e-*fa* when a tritone b-*fa*—e-*mi* is encountered. Discordant intervals are resolved with the least number of adjustments especially where a cadential b-*mi* is found as well. There is a striking change of color in these Mixolydian passages in contrast to the prevailing affect of the sober Dorian melodies and harmonies.

Although almost all linear and harmonic tritones must be adjusted, some diminished fifths are resolved by voice leading, for example in measure 6 of the *Gloria*. Linear tritones require e-*fa*s in both the soprano and tenor parts which sound against a-natural in the alto and bass. The e-*fa* in the soprano resolves by semitone down and the a in the bass resolves up by semitone, to satisfy the ear as a resolution of the discord.

A passage that requires several alterations begins at measure 16 in the *Gloria* that prepares for a cadence to e, the sixth degree of the mode. A minim rest separates b-flat at the end of measure 15 from e-natural at the beginning of measure 16, a tritone that theorists excuse because of the intervening rest. B-*fa* in the tenor is altered to b-*mi* in measure 17, a tritone resolved by semitone to c, to allow a cadence to e-natural in measure 18. This requires the tenor to sing b-*mi* on the first note of measure 18, but such an alteration comes easily to the ear after the preceding e in the soprano. These alterations are much simpler than the succession of flats that would otherwise ensue which would include a-*fas* in measure 18.

In the *Gloria*, linear tritones are altered by a flat in measures 5, 6, 7, 9, 12/13, 14, 15, 20, 21, 29, 33-36, 39/40, 41/42, 67/68, 71/72, and 84/85. They are altered by b-*mi* in measures 23, and 55-58. One linear diminished fifth is corrected by a flat in measure 8. Harmonic tritones are altered by flats in measures 14, 29, and 84, by b-*mi* in measures 18, 25, and 82, and resolved by voice leading in measures 80 and 82. Harmonic diminished fifths are altered by flats in measures 20, 54 and 67, by b-*mi* in measures 17, 18, and 81, and resolved by voice leading in measures 6, 21, 22, 26, 46/47, and 80. Cadences require alterations in measures 10/11, 22, 30/31, 49/50, 64/65/ 79, 82, and 85/86. Other accidentals that are found in the *Gloria* are secondary, in order to avoid augmented or diminished octaves or unpleasant cross relations.

In the *Credo*, linear tritones are altered by flats in measures 5-7, 9, 21, 26-28, 47/48, 67/68, 70, 72, 99-101, 103-105, 113, 136-138, 141/142, 144/145, 146, 148, 177/178, 180, and 185. They are altered by b-*mi* in measures 13, 16, 17, 18/19, 30-32, 40, 76/77, 81-83, 87-91, 126/127, and 128/129. An a-*fa* is suggested in measure 71, which exceeds the rule to limit alterations to one flat beyond the signature, and performers may decide whether or not to sing it. Linear tritones are resolved by voice leading in measures 32 and 80/81, and harmonic diminished fifths are also resolved by voice leading in measures 79/80, 106, and 143. Linear diminished fifths are resolved by flats in measures 2-4, 8, 24, 25, and 31, and by b-*mi* in 122. Harmonic diminished fifths are resolved by flats in measures 26, 29, 63, 65, 74, 95, 109, 144, 150, 162, and 183, and by b-*mi*s in measures 18, 118, 120, and 121. Cadences require alterations in measures 7/8, 11/12, 21/ 22, 44, 55/56, 87, 93/94, 114/115, 119, 123/124, 125/126, 129/130, 140, 154/155, 163/164, and 180/181. No cadential alterations have been suggested in measures 173/174 and 186/187 because of doubled leading tones which suggest that Ockeghem deliberately placed them as obstacles. Performers may decide to overrule this decision and raise both cadential notes.

In the *Sanctus* after measure 17, linear tritones are altered by flats in measures 21, 22, 25, 26, 29/30; in the *Osanna* in measures 3/5, 4/6, 7/9, 14/15, 18/19, 30/31, 36, 37/38; in the *Benedictus* in measures 9/10; and in the *Qui venit* in measures 2, and 28/29. Linear tritones are altered by b-*mi*s in measures 7/8, 11, 13, 15, 21/22, and 28/29 of the *Qui venit*, and three tritones are resolved by voice leading in measure 23 of the

Sanctus, measures 3/4 of the *Benedictus*, and measure 27 of the *Qui venit*. Harmonic tritones are altered in measure 23 of the *Osanna* (with a flat) and measures 11 and 24 of the *Qui venit* (with naturals). Three harmonic tritones are resolved: one with a flat in measure 23 of the *Osanna*, and two with naturals in measures 11 and 24 of the *Qui venit*. Cadential alterations are made in measures 32/33, and 40/41 of the *Osanna*, 12 of the *Benedictus*, 6, 18/19, and 29/30 of the *Qui venit*.

In the *Agnus*, linear tritones are altered in measures 1, 2, 5, 7/8, 9/10, 24-27, 36/37, and 48/49, all with flats with an additional a-flat in measure 9. Harmonic tritones are flatted in measures 20, 21, and 47, and harmonic diminished fifths are flatted in measures 6, 33, and 41. Cadential alterations are found in measures 3/4, 11/12, 15/16, 22/23, 28/29, and 48/49.

Melodic consistency suggests additional alteration in measures 14 and 184 of the *Credo*, 22 and 25 of the *Sanctus*, 8 of the *Osanna*, and 17 and 48 of the *Agnus dei*.

The total number of altered pitches is high in the Dorian mode. There are eighty-two linear tritones altered with a flat, twenty-one altered with a natural, eight linear diminished fifths altered with a flat and one altered with a natural. Nine harmonic tritones are altered with a flat and three with a natural. Twenty-five harmonic diminished fifths are flatted and ten are altered with a natural. There are seven tritones and ten diminished fifths resolved by voice leading. Six a-flats have been introduced, all exceed the rule allowing only one flat beyond the signature. Alternately, the tritones altered by these flats could be allowed to sound. The Dorian version is frequently striking in its contrasts of major and minor intervals, mainly the commixture of Dorian and Mixolydian fifths on g and c, and for this reason numerous phrases of the text are more vividly juxtaposed than in the other modes.

Performance of the *Missa cuiusvis toni* is relatively uncomplicated in the Phrygian and Mixolydian modes. In the Lydian and Dorian modes, Ockeghem's melodic lines frequently revolve around augmented fourths or diminished fifths which increase the number of conflicts of *mi contra fa*. The ability to sing the mass in all modes could have been considered to be be the mark of a well-schooled veteran of solmization in Ockeghem's choir. The singer who thoroughly investigates the solmization technique of this mass will acquire a valuable practical facility as well as insights that can be applied to all music of the 15th and 16th centuries. Modal differences are strikingly perceptible to listeners in versions of this mass, yet they can be subtle in their evocations, sonorities, and in the emphasis placed upon various phrases of the text. Ockeghem's creation is chameleon-like in the colors it takes on in different modes and fascinating both to performers and audience.

Example 2

Example 3 Solmization in Phrygian

Example 4   Solmization in Phrygian

Example 5 Solmization in Mixolydian

Example 6   Solmization in Mixolydian

Example 7   Solmization in Lydian

Example 8 Solmization in Lydian

Example 9 Solmization in Dorian

Example 10 Solmization in Dorian

Phrygian

Kyrie

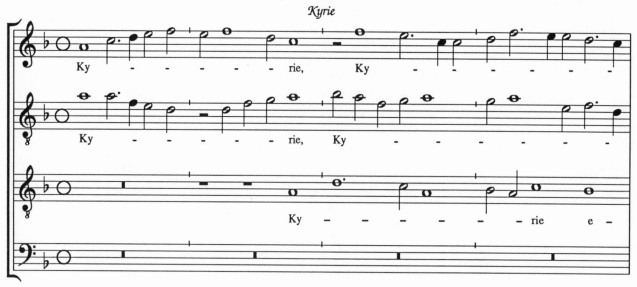

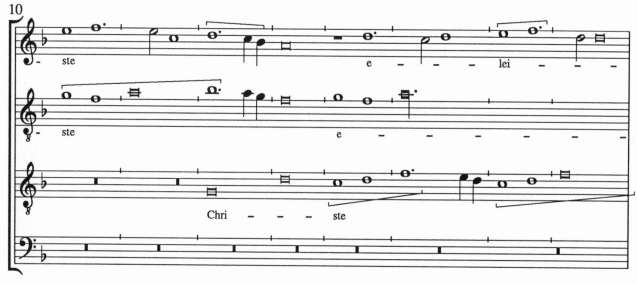

Kyrie

Gloria

Gloria

Gloria

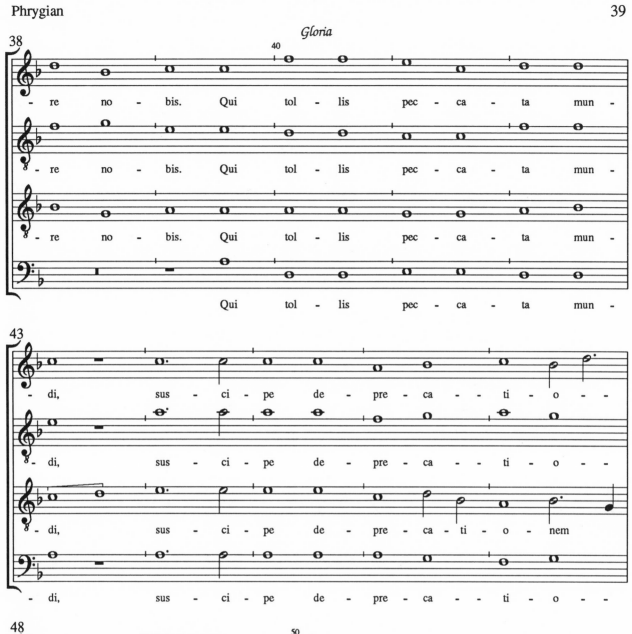

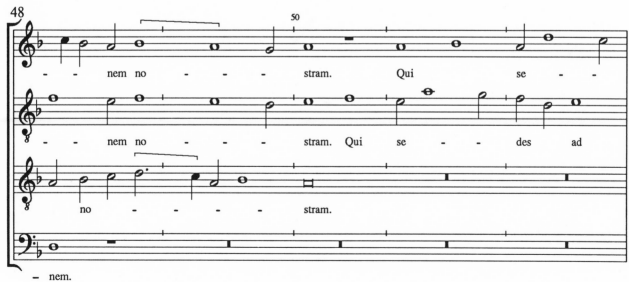

Gloria

53

-des   ad   dex-te-ram   Pa   -   -   tris,   mi - se -

dex-te-ram Pa - - tris, mi-se - re - re

mi - se - re -

ad   dex - te - ram Pa - - tris,

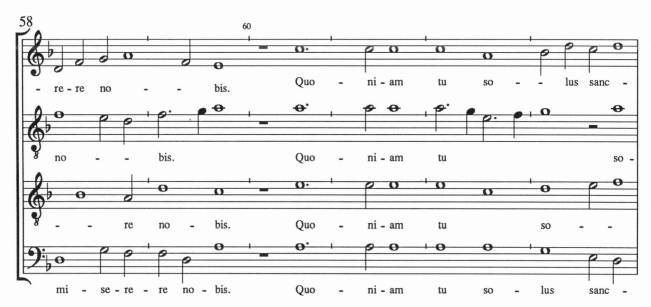

58   60

-re-re no - - bis.   Quo - ni-am tu so - lus sanc -

no - - bis.   Quo - ni-am tu   so -

- re no - bis.   Quo - ni-am tu   so -

mi - se - re - re no - bis.   Quo - ni-am tu so - lus sanc -

64

- - tus,   tu so - lus Do - mi - ne, tu so - lus al - tis - si -

- lus sanc - tus,   tu so - lus al - tis - si - mus,

- lus sanc - - tus,   tu so - lus al -

- - tus,   tu so - lus Do - mi - nus

Gloria

Credo in unumDeum

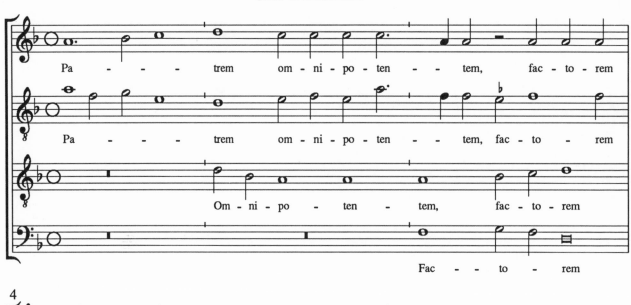

Credo

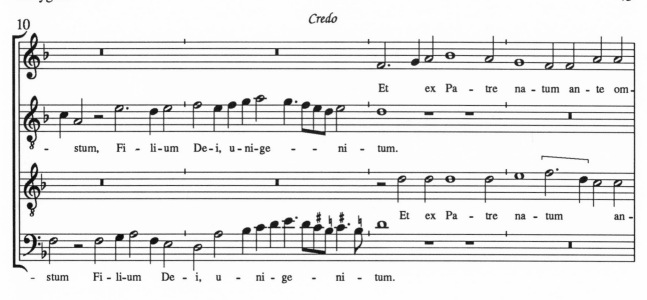

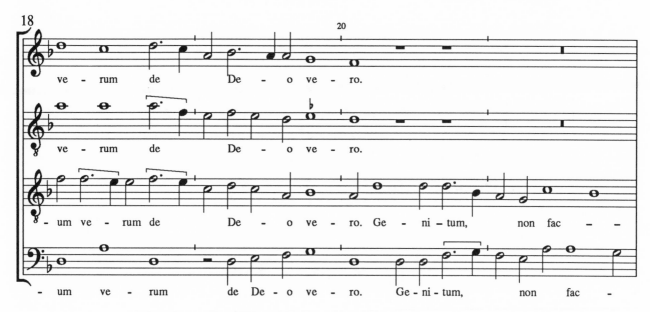

Credo

Credo

Credo

Credo

Credo

Credo

Credo

Credo

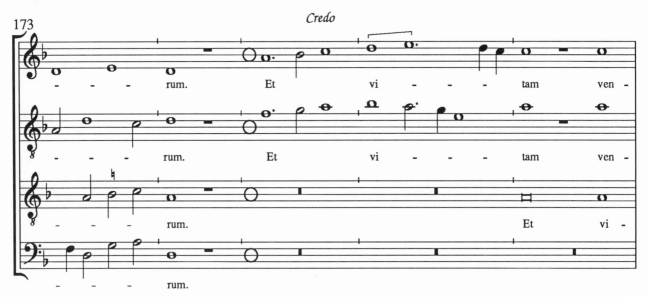

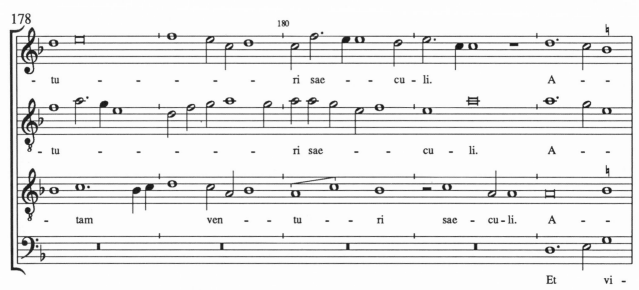

Sanctus

Sanctus

Sanctus

Sanctus

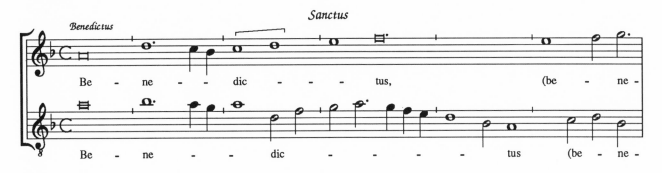

Benedictus

Be — ne — dic — — tus, (be — ne —

Be — ne — — dic — — — tus (be — ne —

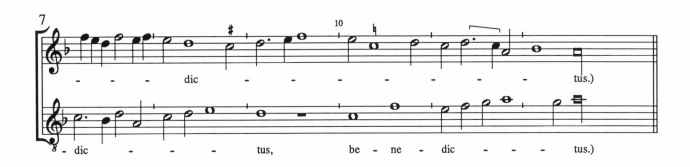

— — dic — — — — — — — — — tus.)

— dic — — — tus, be — ne — dic — — tus.)

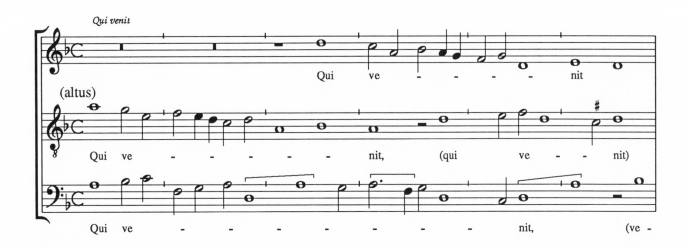

Qui venit

Qui ve — — — — nit nit

(altus)

Qui ve — — — — nit, (qui ve — nit)

Qui ve — — — — — — — nit, (ve —

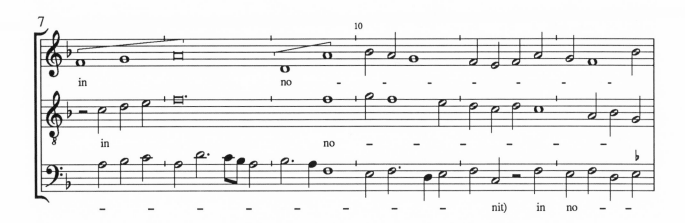

in   no — — — — — — — —

in   no — — — — — — —

— — — — — — — — — nit) in no — —

Sanctus

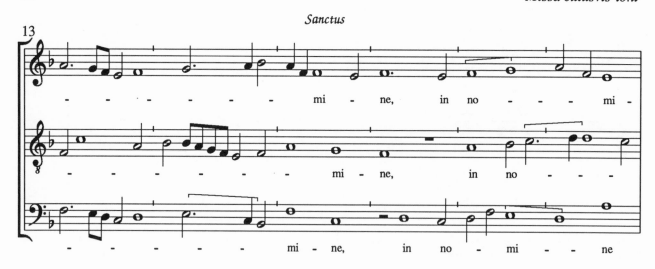

Osanna ut supra

Agnus dei

Agnus dei

Agnus dei

Agnus dei I ut supra

Mixolydian

Kyrie

Missa cuiusvis toni

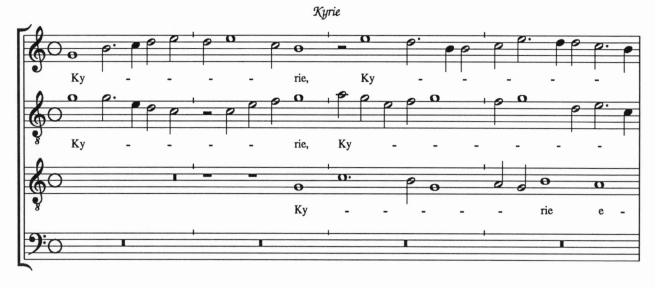

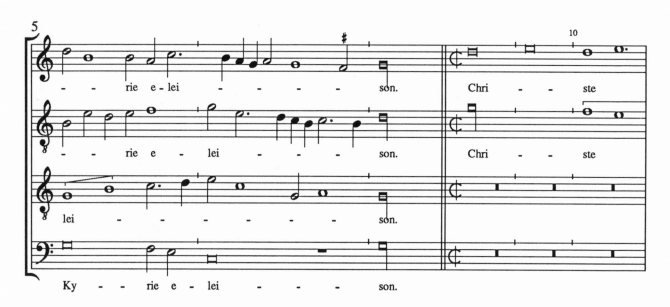

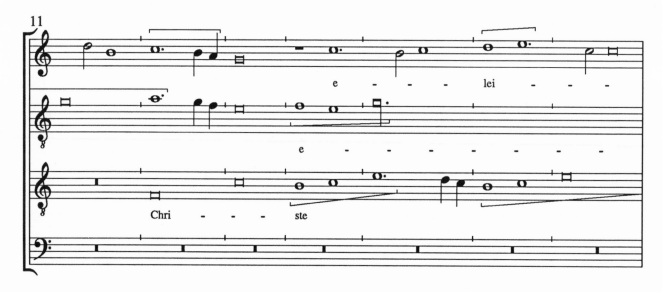

Kyrie

Gloria

Gloria

Gloria

Gloria

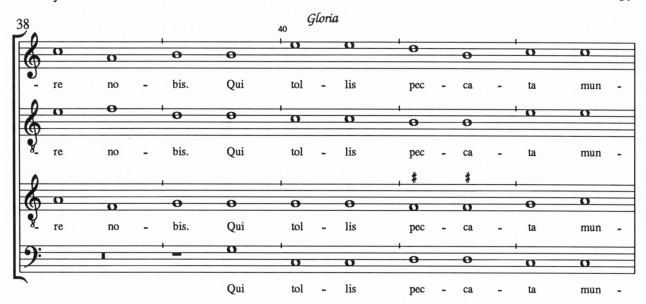

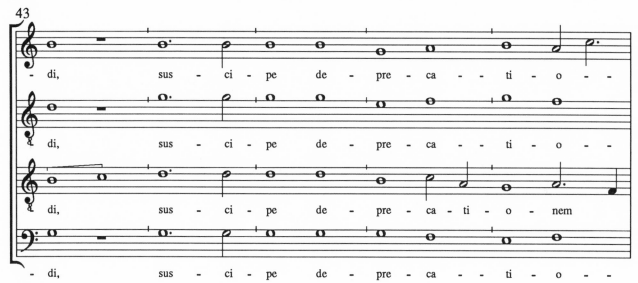

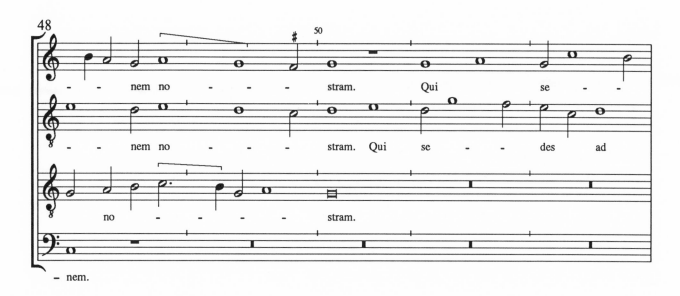

Gloria

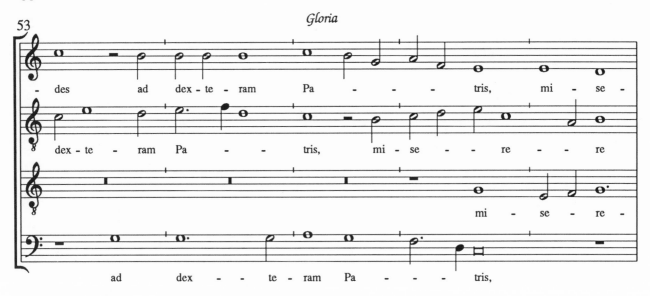

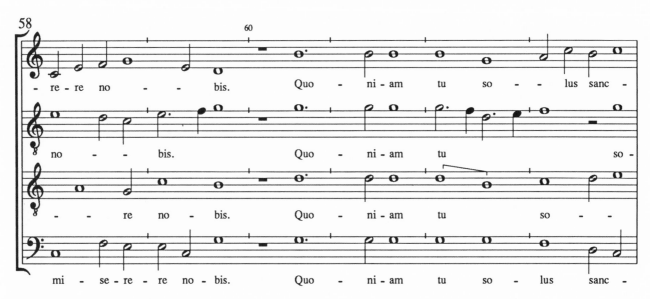

Gloria

Credo in unum Deum

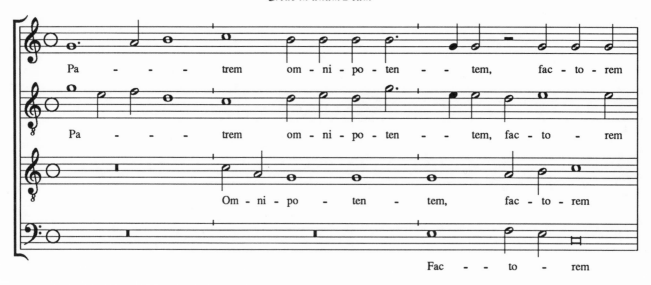

Credo

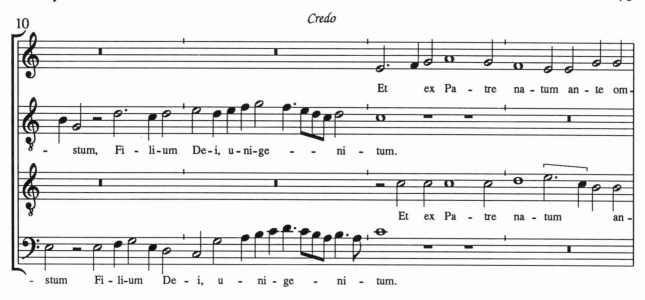

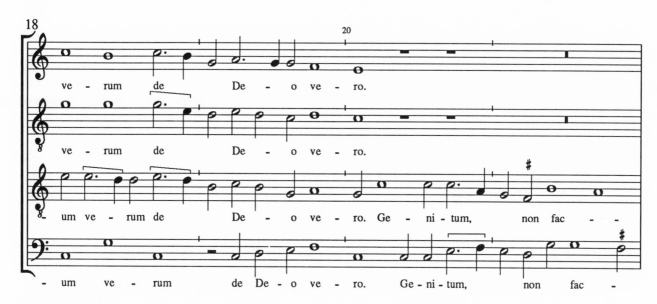

Credo

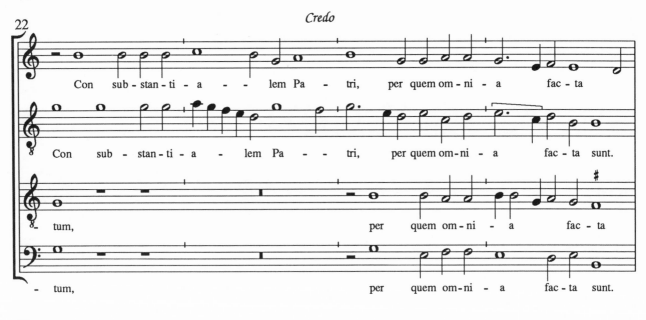

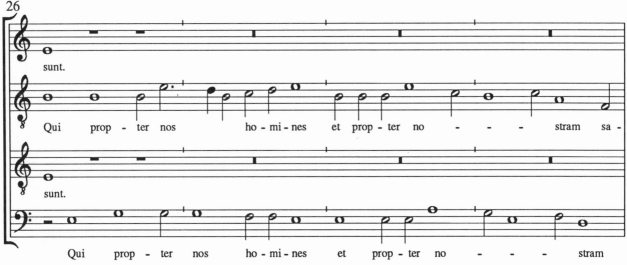

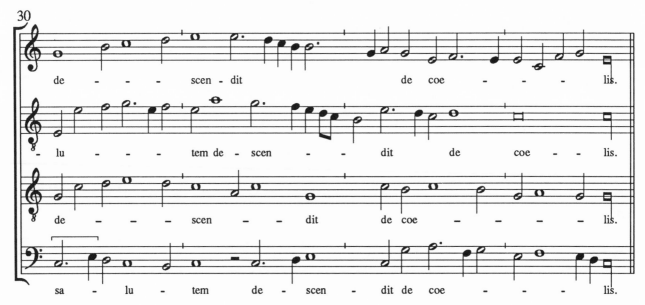

Credo

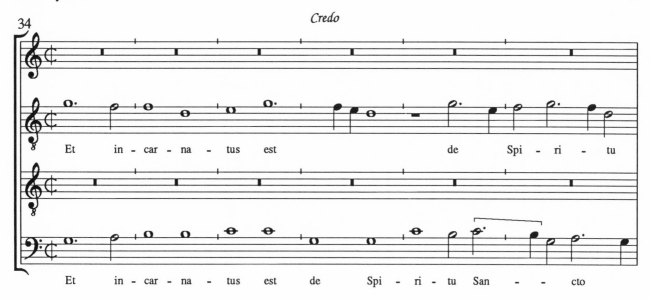

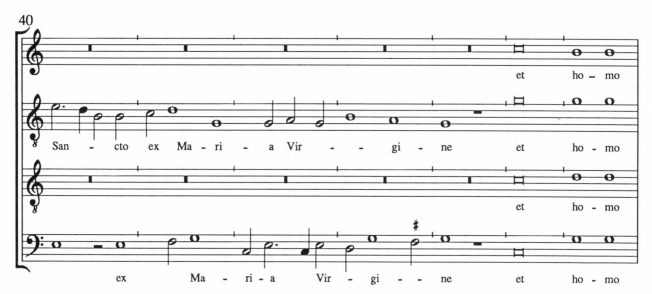

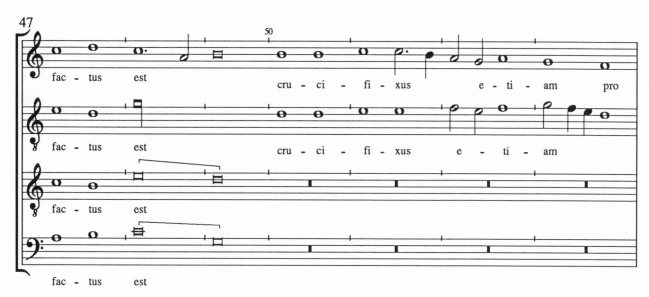

Credo

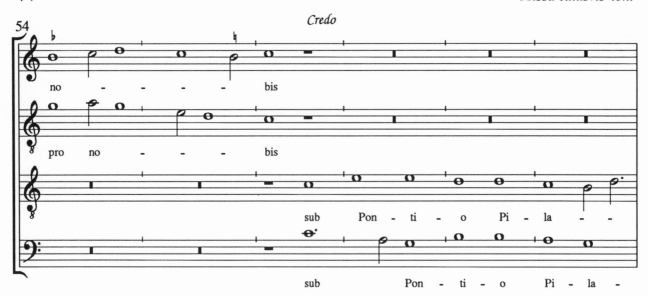

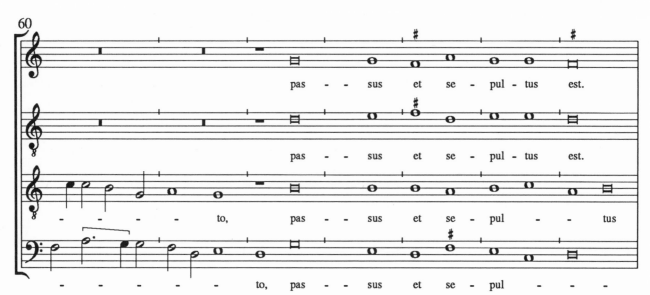

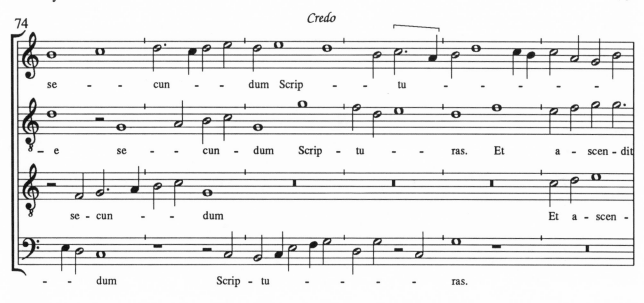

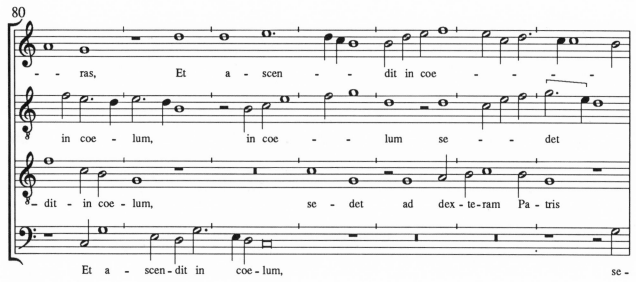

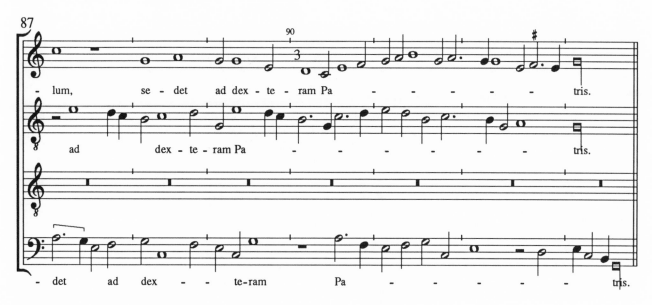

Credo

Credo

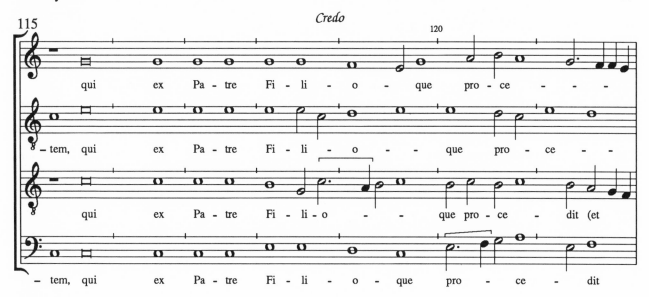

qui ex Pa - tre Fi - li - o - que pro ce - -

- tem, qui ex Pa - tre Fi - li - o - - que pro - ce -

qui ex Pa - tre Fi - li - o - - que pro-ce - dit (et

- tem, qui ex Pa - tre Fi - li - o - que pro - ce - dit

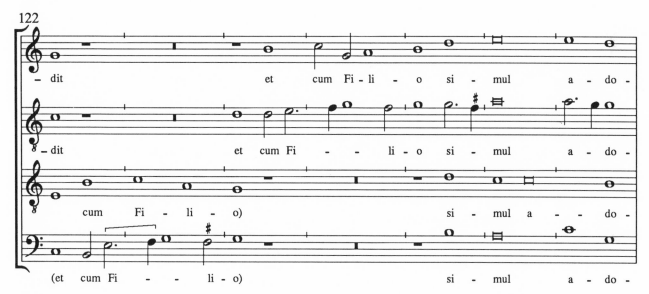

- dit et cum Fi - li - o si - mul a - do -

- dit et cum Fi - - li - o si - mul a - do -

cum Fi - li - o) si - mul a - do -

(et cum Fi - - li - o) si - mul a - do -

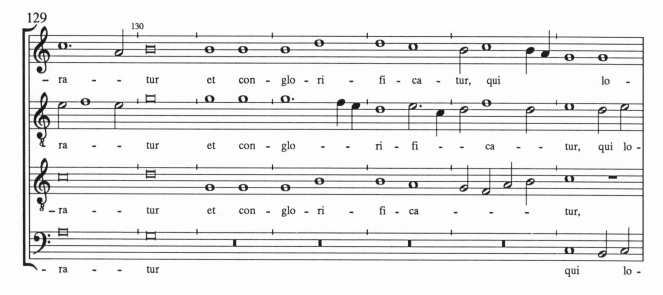

- ra - tur et con - glo - ri - fi - ca - tur, qui lo -

- ra - tur et con - glo - ri - fi - ca - tur, qui lo -

- ra - tur et con - glo - ri - fi - ca - - tur,

- ra - tur qui lo -

Credo

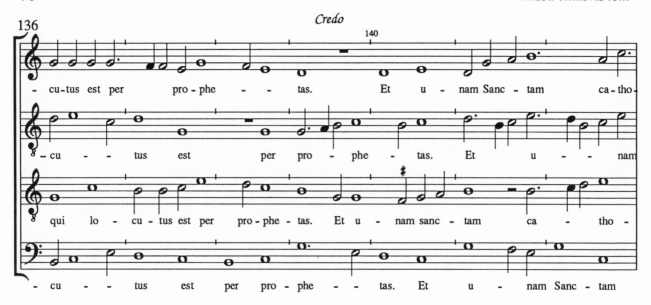

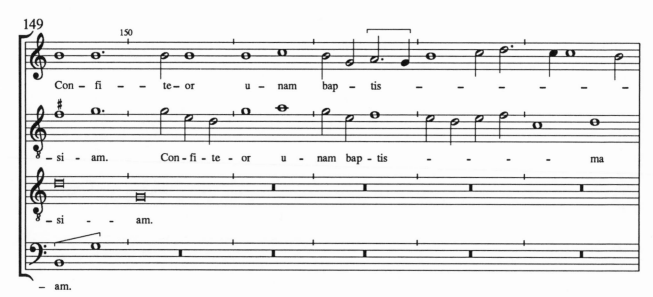

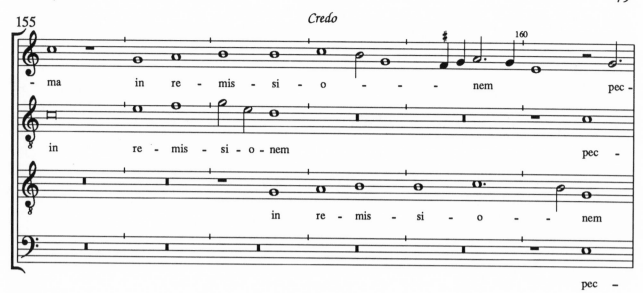

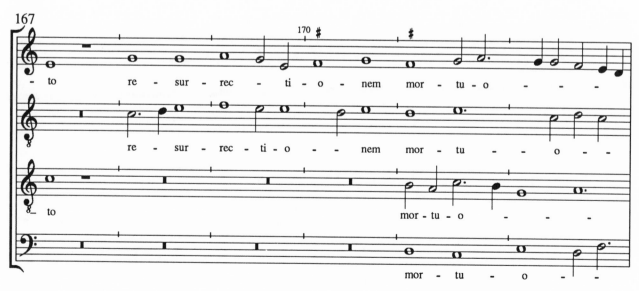

Credo

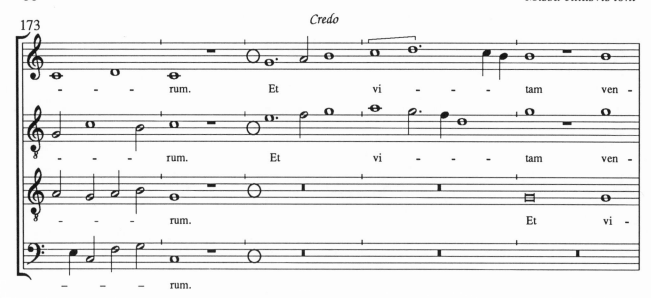

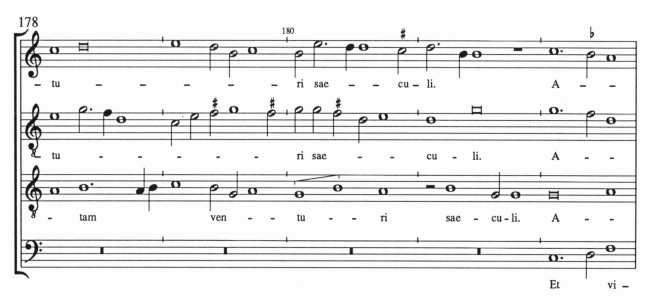

Sanctus

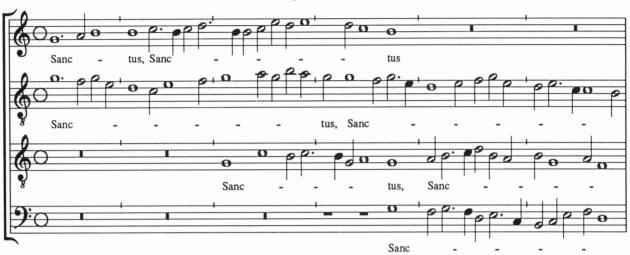

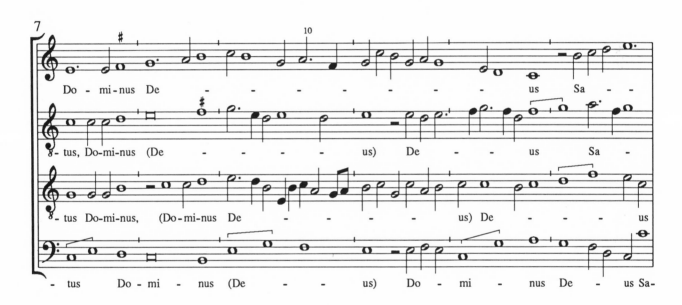

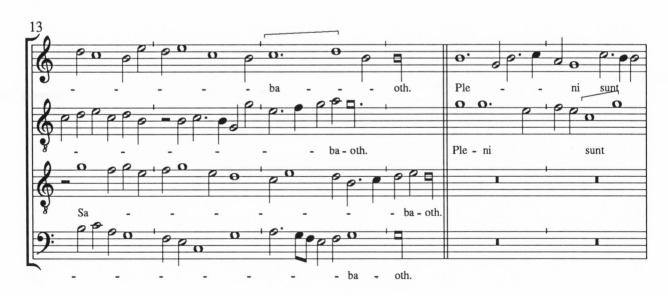

Sanctus

Sanctus

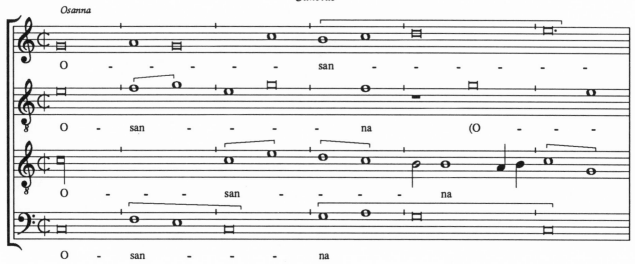

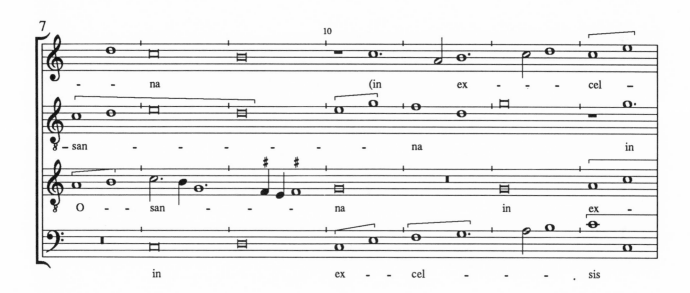

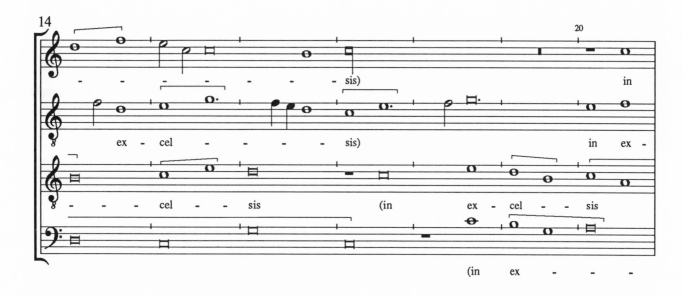

Sanctus

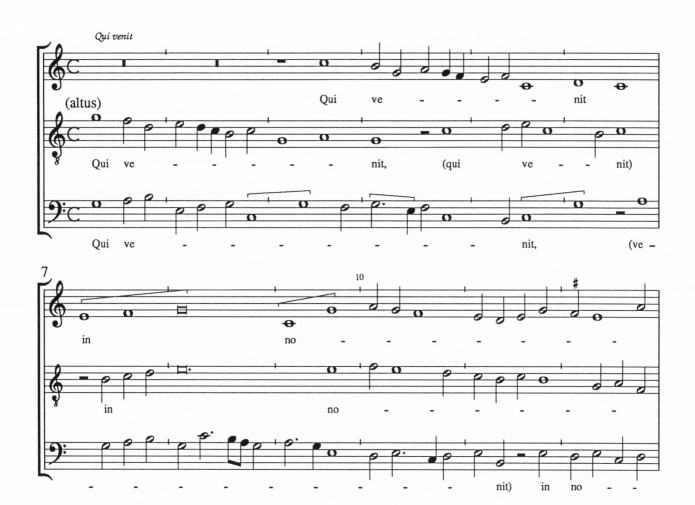

Sanctus

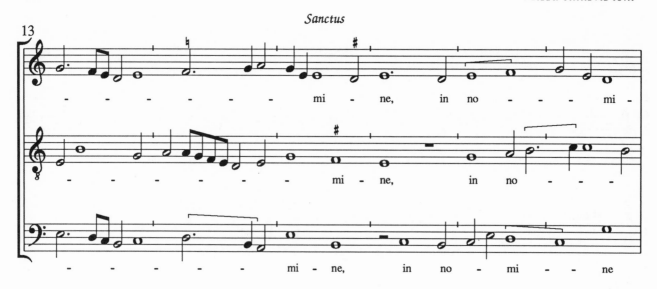

Osanna ut supra

Agnus dei

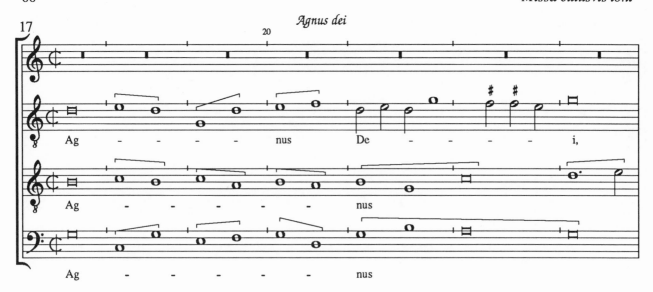

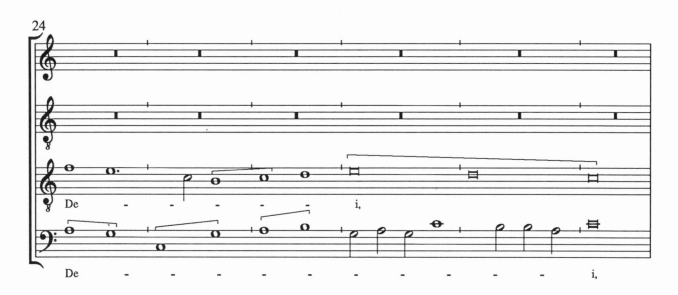

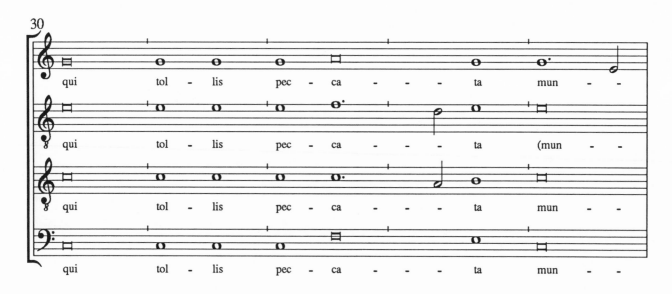

Agnus dei

Agnus dei I ut supra

Lydian
Kyrie

Ky - - - - rie, Ky - - - - - - -

Ky - - - - rie, Ky - - - - - -

Ky - - - - - rie e -

- - rie e - lei - - - - son. Chri - - ste

- - rie e - lei - - - son. Chri - - ste

lei - - - - - - - son.

Ky - - rie e - lei - - - son.

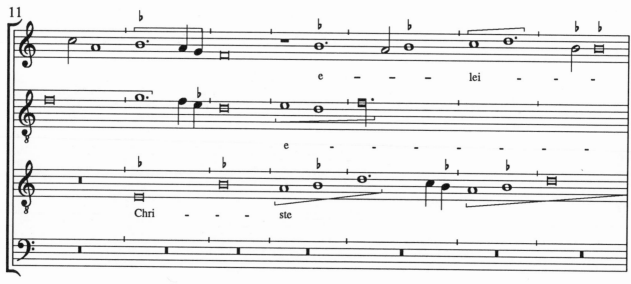

e - - - lei - - -

e - - -

Chri - - - ste

Gloria

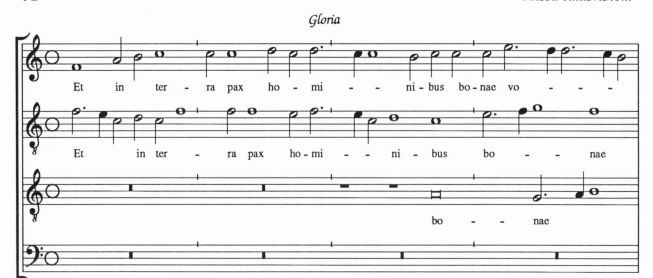

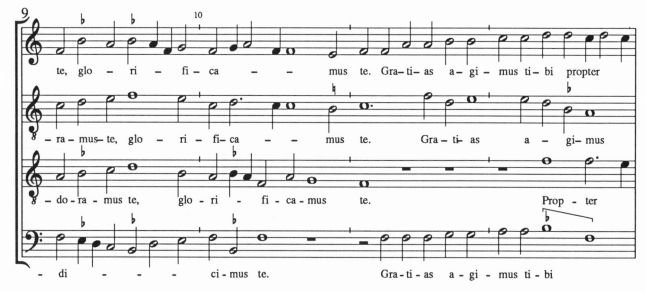

Gloria

Gloria

Credo in unum Deum

Credo

Credo

Credo

Credo

Credo

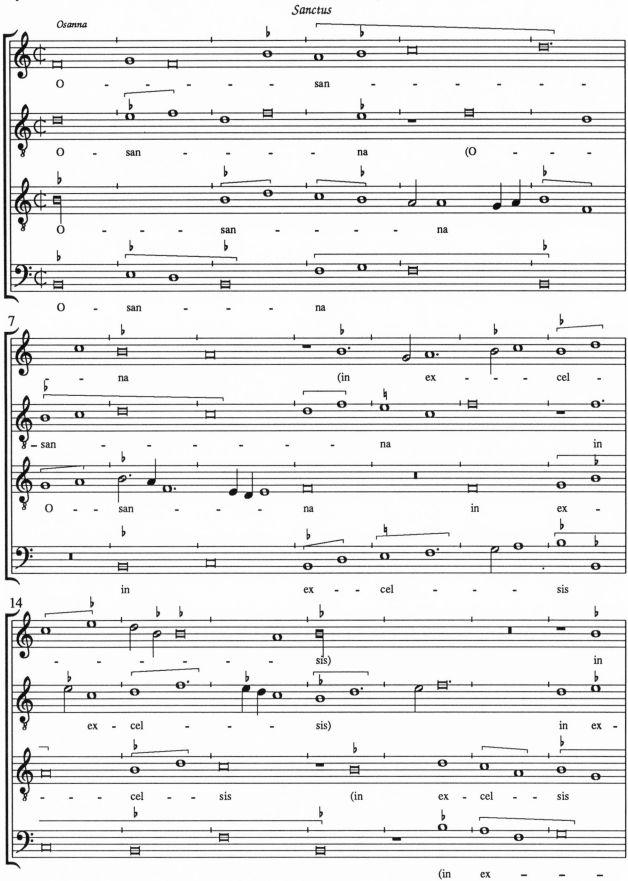

Sanctus

Sanctus

Osanna ut supra

Agnus dei

Agnus dei

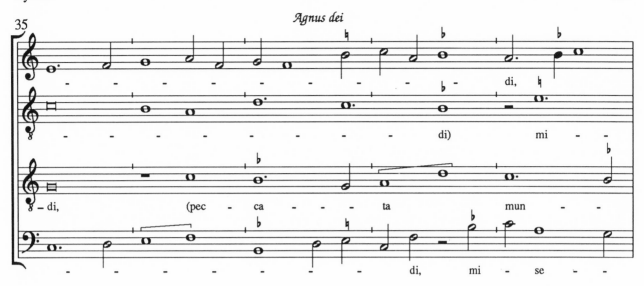

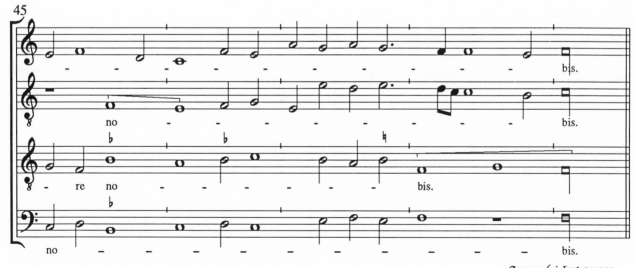

Agnus dei I ut supra

Dorian
Kyrie

Kyrie

Gloria

Gloria

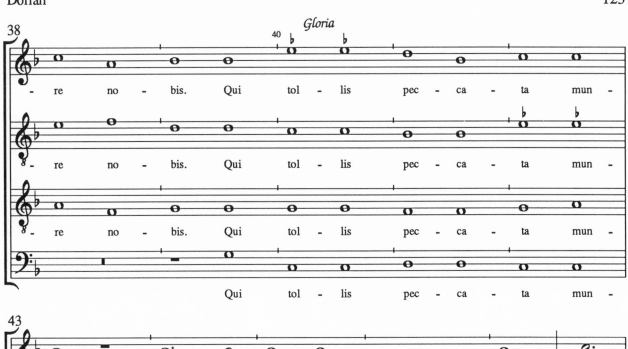

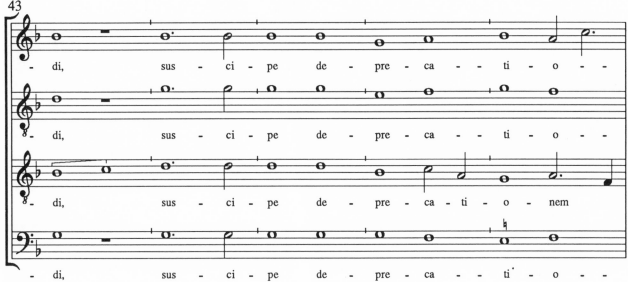

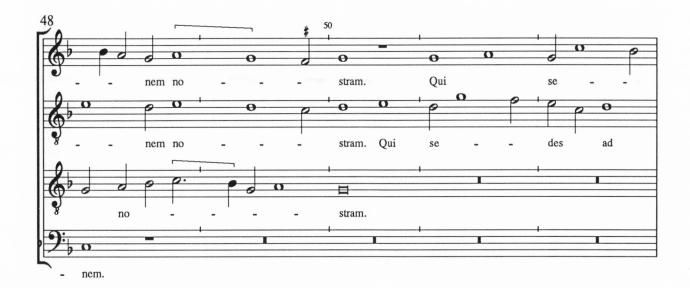

Gloria

Gloria

Credo in unum Deum

Credo

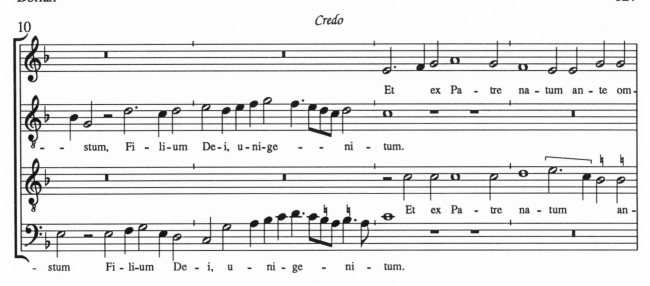

Credo

Credo

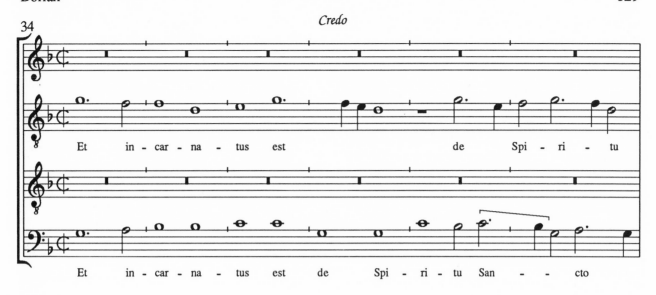

Et in-car-na-tus est   de   Spi - ri - tu

Et   in-car-na - tus   est   de   Spi - ri - tu San - cto

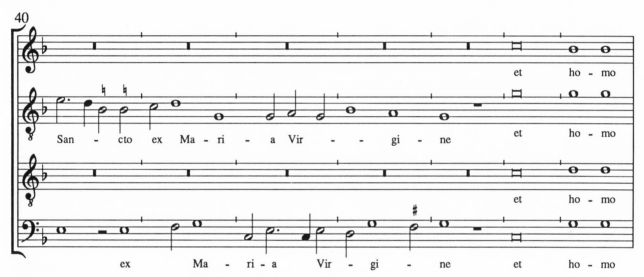

et   ho - mo

San - cto ex Ma - ri - a Vir - gi - ne   et   ho - mo

et   ho - mo

ex   Ma - ri - a Vir - gi - ne   et   ho - mo

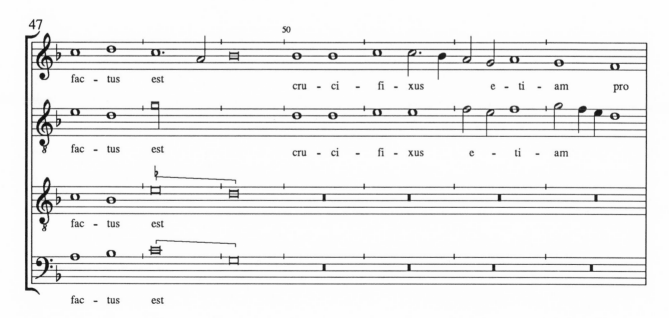

fac - tus   est   cru - ci - fi - xus   e - ti - am   pro

fac - tus   est   cru - ci - fi - xus   e - ti - am

fac - tus   est

fac - tus   est

Credo

Credo

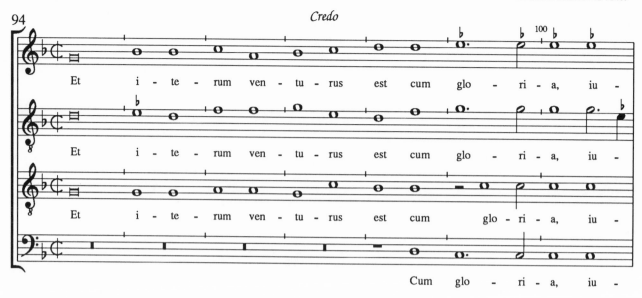

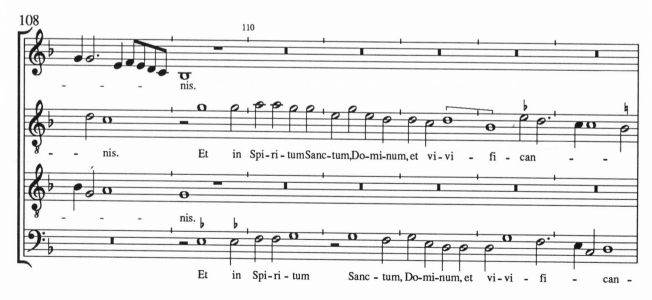

Credo

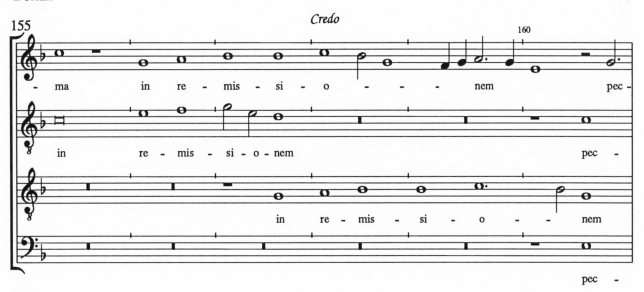

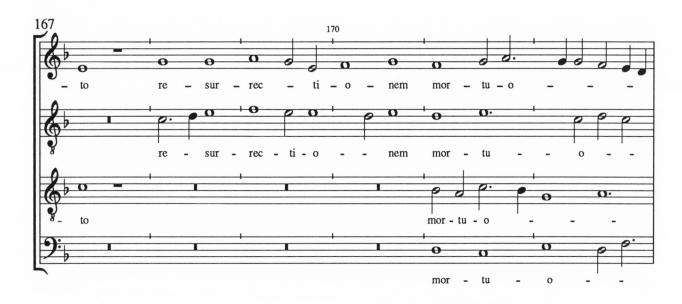

Credo

Sanctus

Sanctus

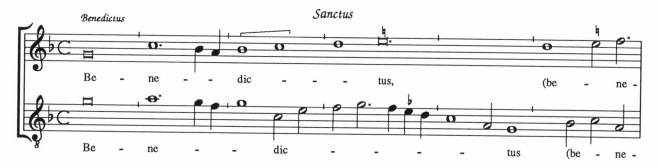

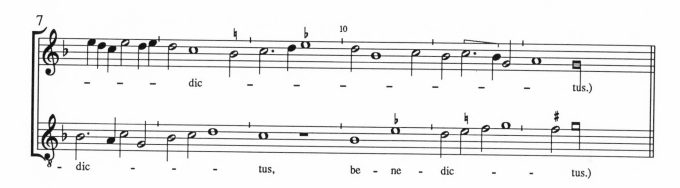

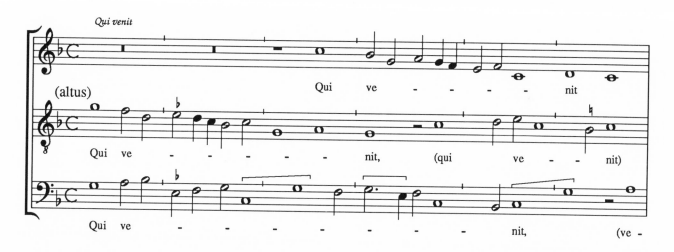

Sanctus

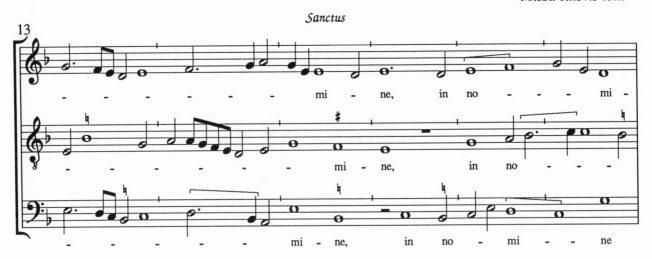

Osanna ut supra

Agnus dei

Agnus dei

Agnus dei I ut supra